260
DRUM MACHINE
PATTERNS

By RENÉ-PIERRE BARDET

T0057160

Contents

ISBN 978-0-88188-887-4

HAL•LEONARD®
CORPORATION
7777 W. BLUEMOUND RD. P.O. BOX 13819 MILWAUKEE, WI 53213

Preface

This book is a supplement to the first volume of DRUM MACHINE PATTERNS. In it you'll find over 260 rhythm patterns and breaks, or fills. These are original patterns that can be programmed easily on any drum machine.

This book, like its predecessor, contains the rhythms most often used in contemporary music.

The easiest way to use the patterns in these two volumes is to store them in groups. For example, program all the Rock patterns and breaks into your drum machine, and then save them using the cassette or MIDI interface provided for external storage. Do this for each rhythm (Rock, Pop, Funk, etc.). This requires a certain investment of time at the start but will come in handy later. Thus, when you have to work on a Funk piece, for example, you can load all of the appropriate rhythms and breaks into your drum machine at one time. This gives you a considerable range of patterns ready to use immediately.

Feel free to modify the patterns in this book to suit your taste, inspiration, or whim. They constitute a solid and efficient base of current rhythms from which you can work.

Explanations

The rhythms are listed in alphabetical order, with corresponding breaks.

As in the first volume, patterns are presented both in musical notation and in "step time" grids. To help you program the patterns easily, numbers appear above the grids to show the subdivisions of the measure.

Some drum machines are capable of several different levels of accents. The use of these different levels, if your machine possesses them, is left to your discretion.

Tempos are left up to you.

One recent innovation in drum machines that makes its appearance in this book is the "flam." A flam is a note that is struck just before the principal beat. A flam is indicated by a grace note in the musical notation, and by an "F" preceding the note to be played in the grid.

You'll find a blank pattern sheet at the end of the book, which you can photocopy and use in notating patterns of your own.

Abbreviations

Following are the abbreviations for the various elements that constitute the "drum set" found in drum machines.

AC: Accent	CH: Closed Hi-Hat
BD: Bass Drum	OH: Open Hi-Hat
SD: Snare Drum	CY: Cymbal
LT: Low Tom	RS: Rim Shot
MT: Medium Tom	CPS: Claps
HT: High Tom	CB: Cowbell
TAM: Tambourine	

Grid Notation

The grid below is typical of those found in this book.

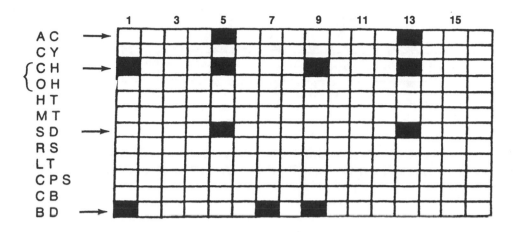

- **Each grid represents a one-measure drum pattern.**

- **Each row of boxes in the grid represents one of the instruments in the drum set. An arrow is placed next to each instrument that is used in that particular pattern. Thus, you can ignore the lines without arrows.**

- **Each box in a row represents a unit of time. This unit is a sixteenth note (♪) or a sixteenth rest (𝄾), depending on whether the box is black (note) or white (rest).**

Most patterns are in 4/4 time, as the example is. This means there are four quarter notes (♩) in a measure. The sixteenth-note unit used by drum machines allows each beat to be broken into four subdivisions. In simple mathematics:

- **A quarter note is a quarter of a measure.**

- **A sixteenth note is a quarter of a quarter note, or a sixteenth of a measure.**

A rhythm pattern in 4/4 time, such as that in the example, will therefore have 16 boxes in each row.

Because the sounds in a drum machine have a fixed duration (you can't play a "long note" on a snare drum; all you can do is hit it), the grids do not show the length of a drum sound. Rather, they show only the places where each drum is "hit."

Musical Notation

The literal translation of the grid in the example into musical notation would be as follows:

literal notation

Since this involves many short rests, however, common practice takes liberties with the notation, substituting longer note values for greater clarity:

common notation

The following key shows how each element of the drum set is notated on the musical staff.

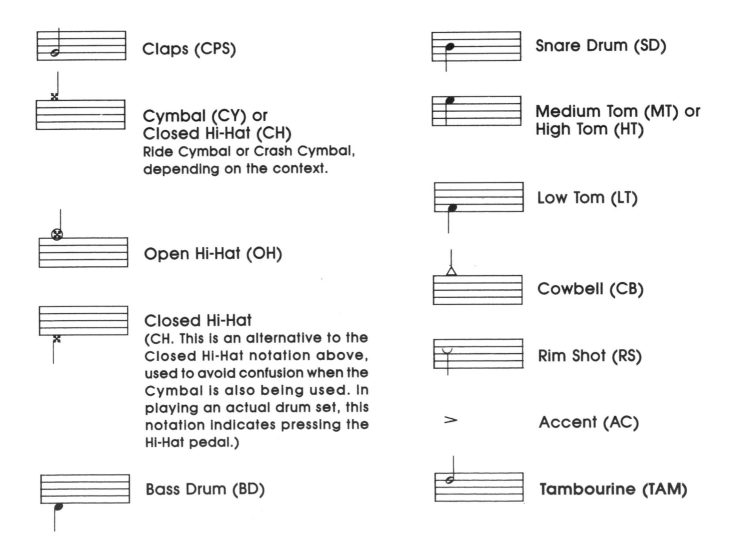

Claps (CPS)

Cymbal (CY) or
Closed Hi-Hat (CH)
Ride Cymbal or Crash Cymbal, depending on the context.

Open Hi-Hat (OH)

Closed Hi-Hat
(CH. This is an alternative to the Closed Hi-Hat notation above, used to avoid confusion when the Cymbal is also being used. In playing an actual drum set, this notation indicates pressing the Hi-Hat pedal.)

Bass Drum (BD)

Snare Drum (SD)

Medium Tom (MT) or
High Tom (HT)

Low Tom (LT)

Cowbell (CB)

Rim Shot (RS)

Accent (AC)

Tambourine (TAM)

How To Use This Book

1. Carefully read the user's manual for your drum machine in order to learn how to operate it in the WRITE (program rhythms) and the PLAY (listen to programmed rhythms) modes.

2. If you've chosen to program a pattern that is 16 units long (4/4 time; e.g., Rock or Pop), it is shown here by a grid that is 16 boxes across. If, on the other hand, you have chosen to program a 12-unit pattern(12/8 time, or 4/4 time with triplets; e.g., Blues or Shuffle), it is shown here by a grid that is 12 boxes across, and each box represents an eighth note rather than a sixteenth note. Select the appropriate pattern length on your drum machine.

3. Activate the WRITE mode.

   Using the example:

   a) Program AC (Accent):

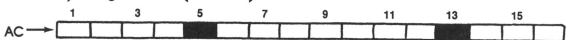

   4 silences – 1 note – 7 silences – 1 note - 3 silences

   (4 + 1 + 7 + 1 + 3 = 16)

   b) Program CH (Closed High-Hat):

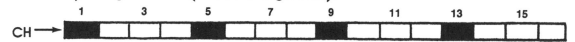

   1 note – 3 silences – 1 note – 3 silences – 1 note – 3 silences – 1 note – 3 silences

   (1 + 3 + 1 + 3 + 1 + 3 + 1+ 3 = 16)

   c) Program SD (Snare Drum):

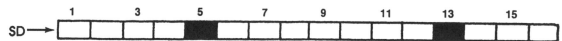

   4 silences – 1 note – 7 silences – 1 note – 3 silences

   (4 + 1 + 7 + 1 + 3 = 16)

   d) Program BD (Bass Drum):

   1 note – 5 silences – 1 note – 1 silence – 1 note – 7 silences

   (1 + 5 + 1 + 1 + 1 + 7 = 16)

4. Switch to PLAY mode and listen to the rhythm.

5. Adjust the tempo to your taste.

Using The Patterns

You've just programmed a one-measure rhythm pattern. But one pattern playing continuously would quickly become boring. So drum machines have what is called "song mode," or "chain mode," which allows you to string several patterns together to form a more interesting whole.

To use song mode, you would first program a minimum of two complementary patterns, and perhaps a break. In a typical song, the main patterns alternate, and the break occurs in the last measure of the phrase (phrases usually are 8 or 16 measures long). For example:

1 + 2 + 1 + 2 + 1 + 2 + 1 + Break

or 1 + 1 + 2 + 2 + 1 + 1 + 2 + Break

The cymbal parts, which have been indicated for Closed Hi-Hat (CH), you may wish to program for the Cymbal (sometimes called "Ride Cymbal"; CY). You may also wish to add Claps (CPS) or High Tom (HT) to underscore accents, and so on, keeping in mind, obviously, the capabilities of your machine.

This book is absolutely not a substitute for your imagination. It is designed to help you in putting basic rhythms into place, but it's up to you to personalize them. An infinite variety of rhythmic combinations lies at your disposal.

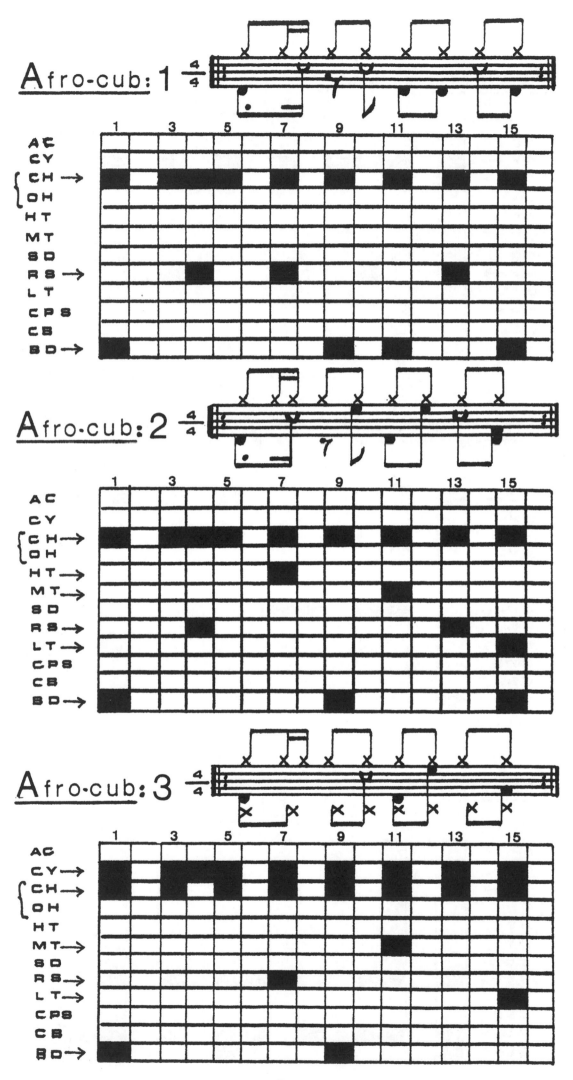

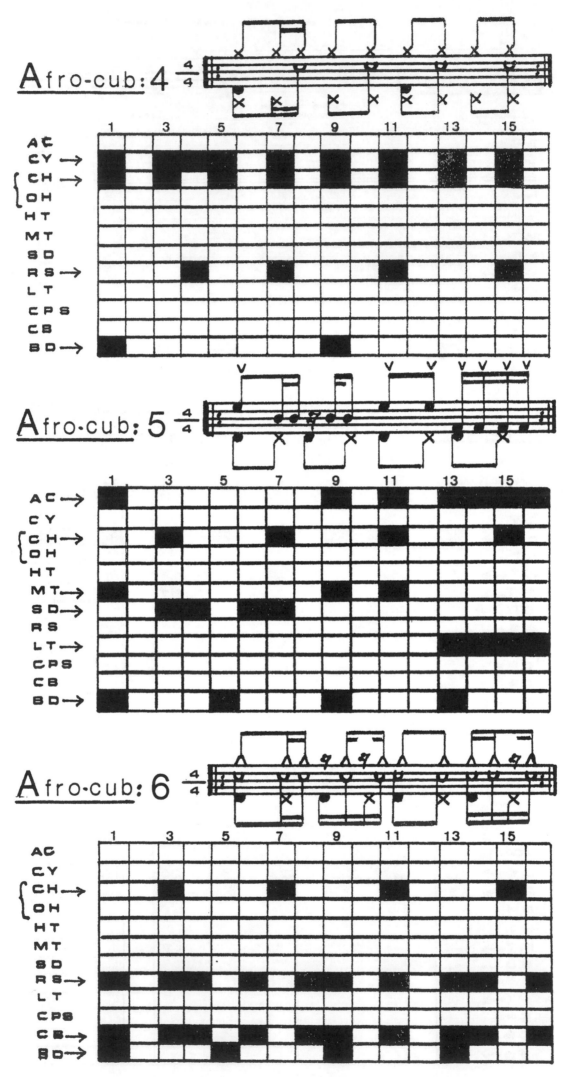

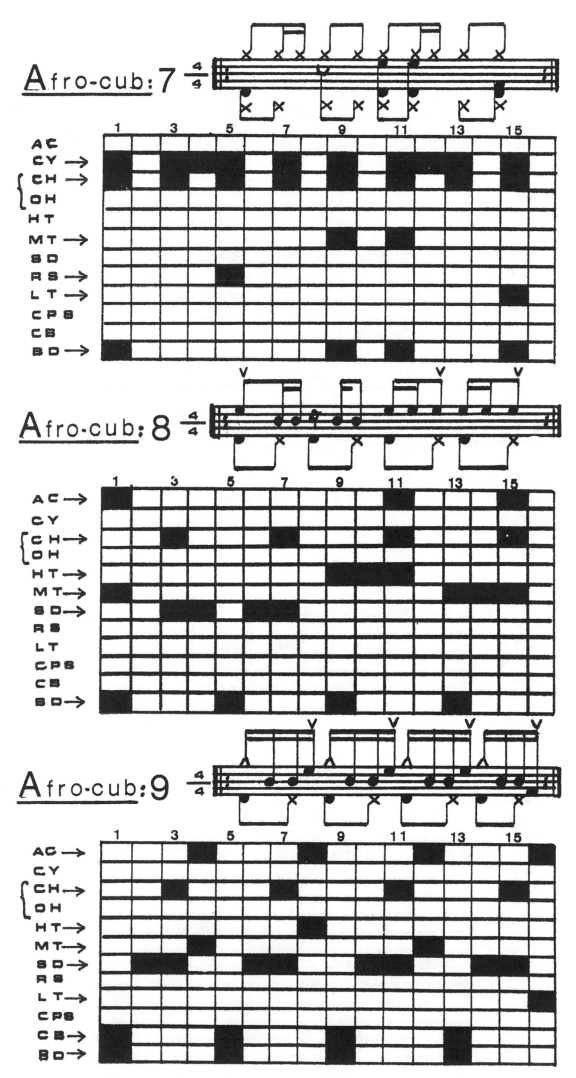

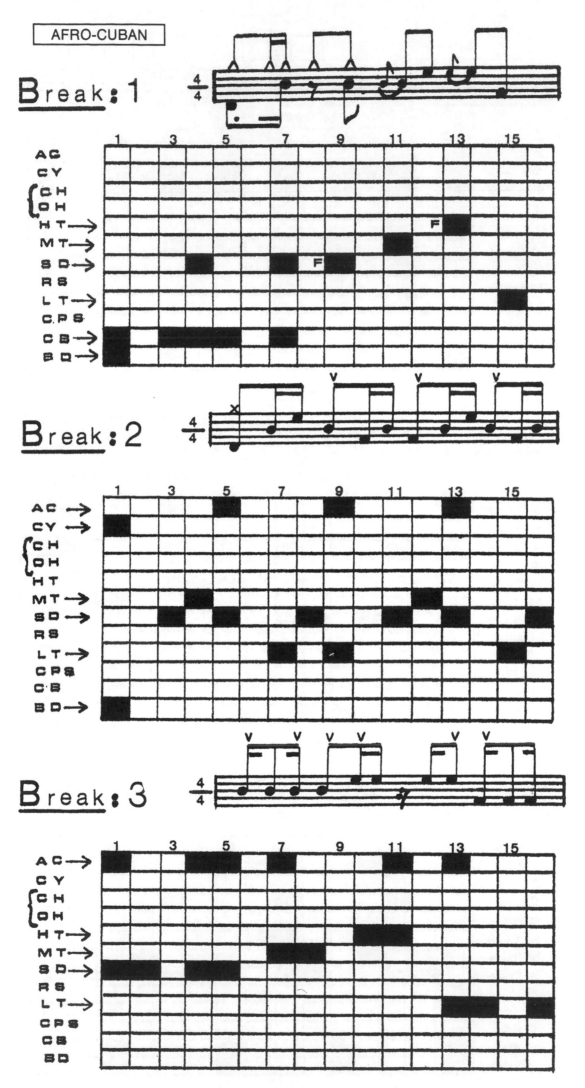

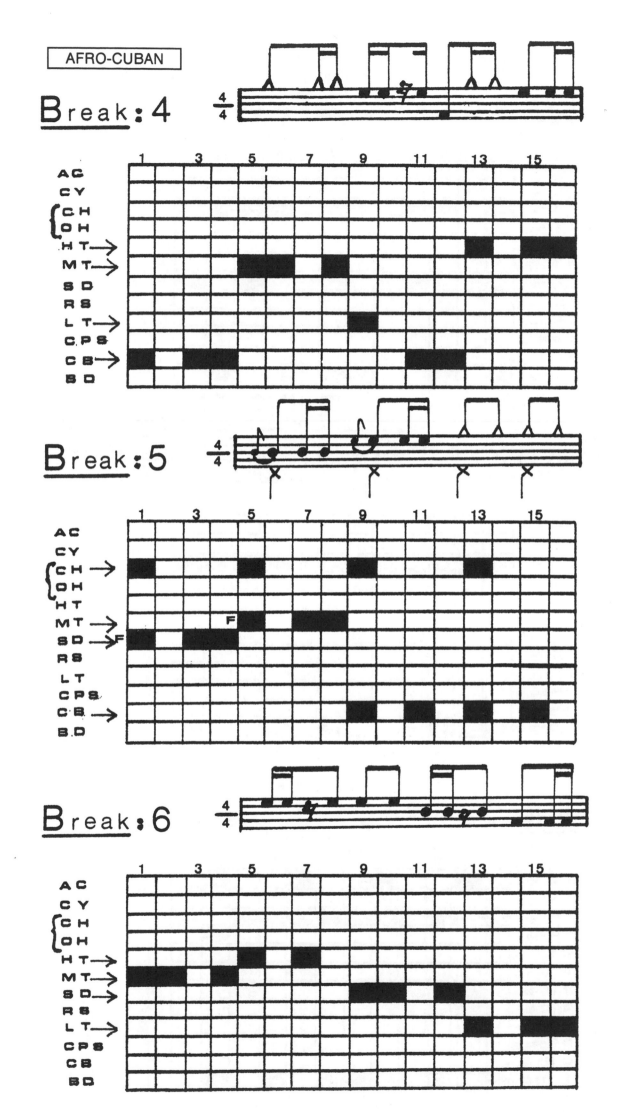

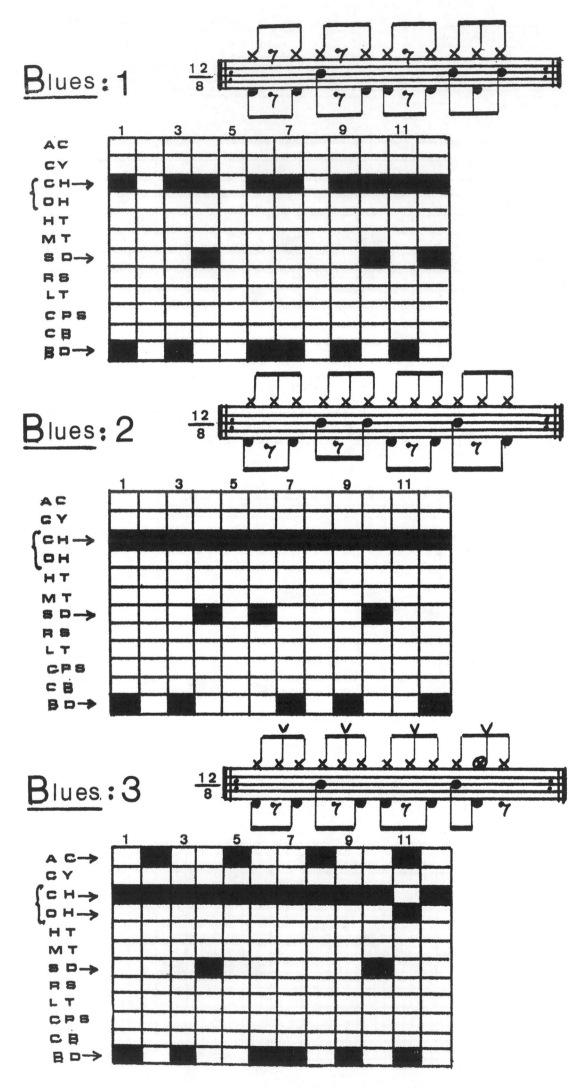

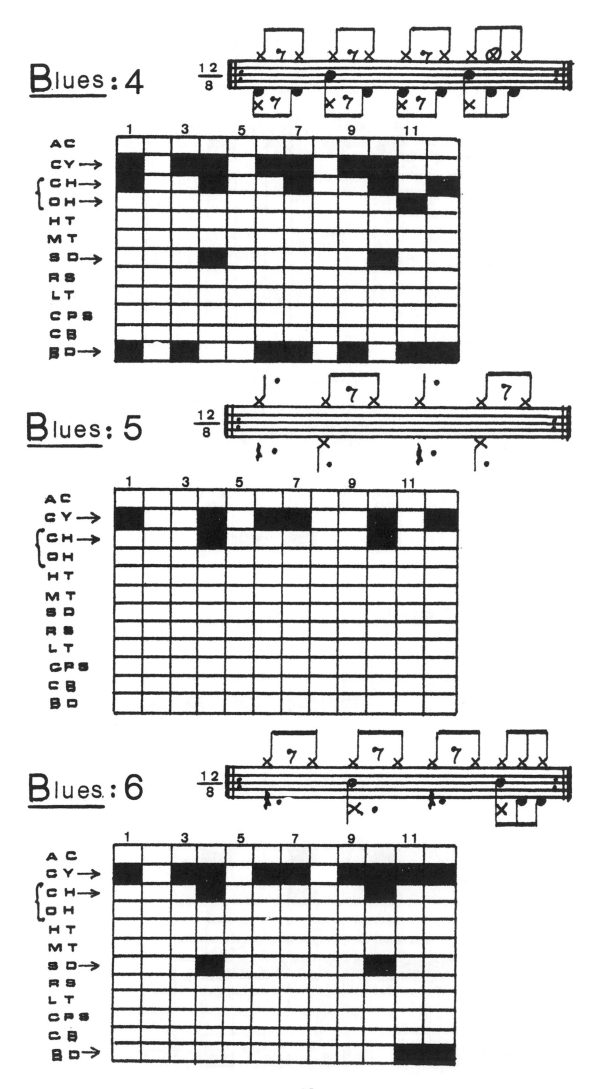

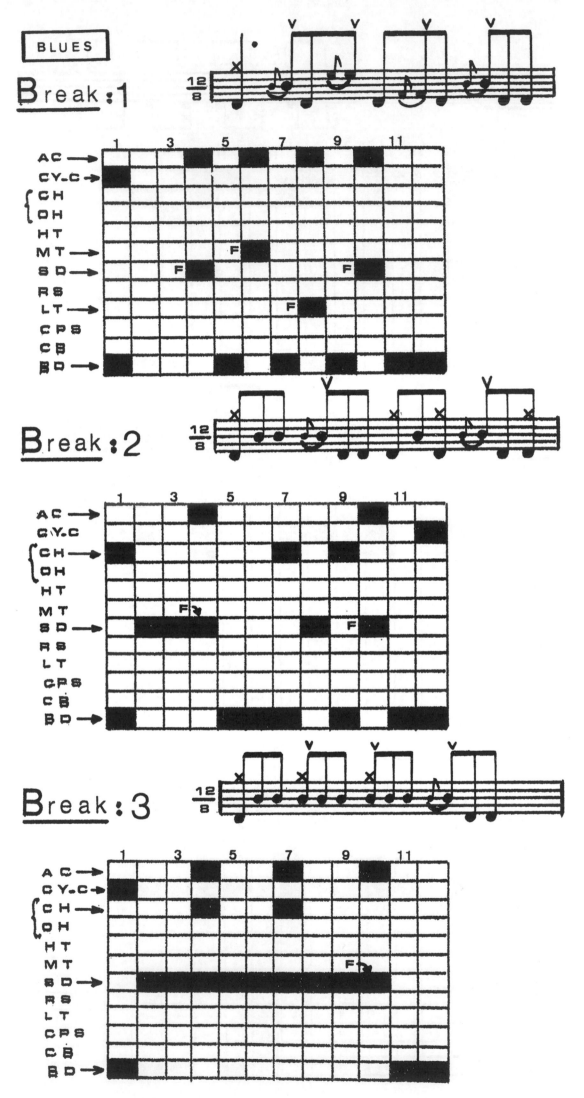

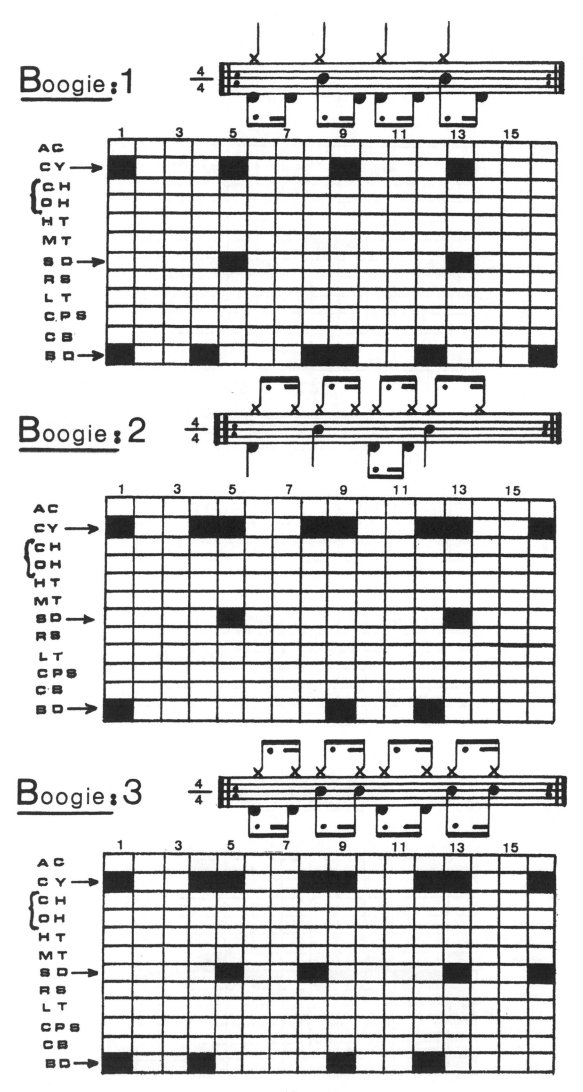

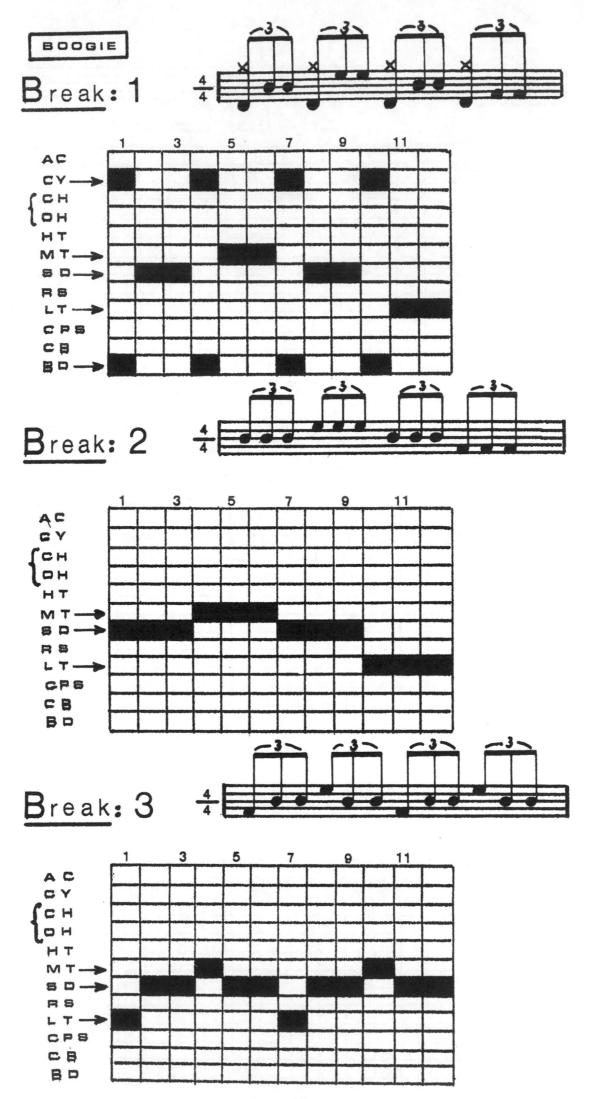

16

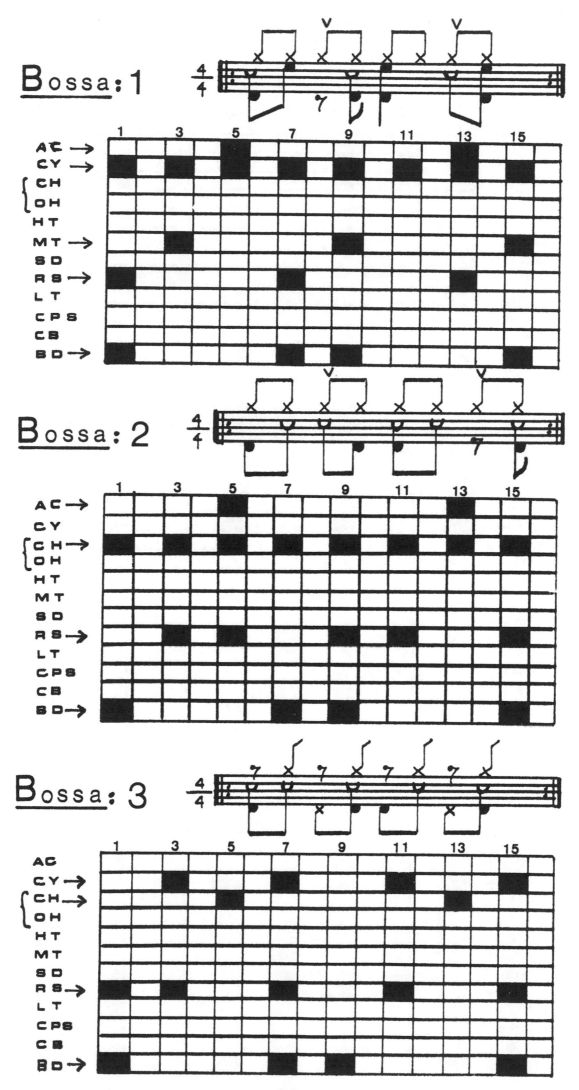

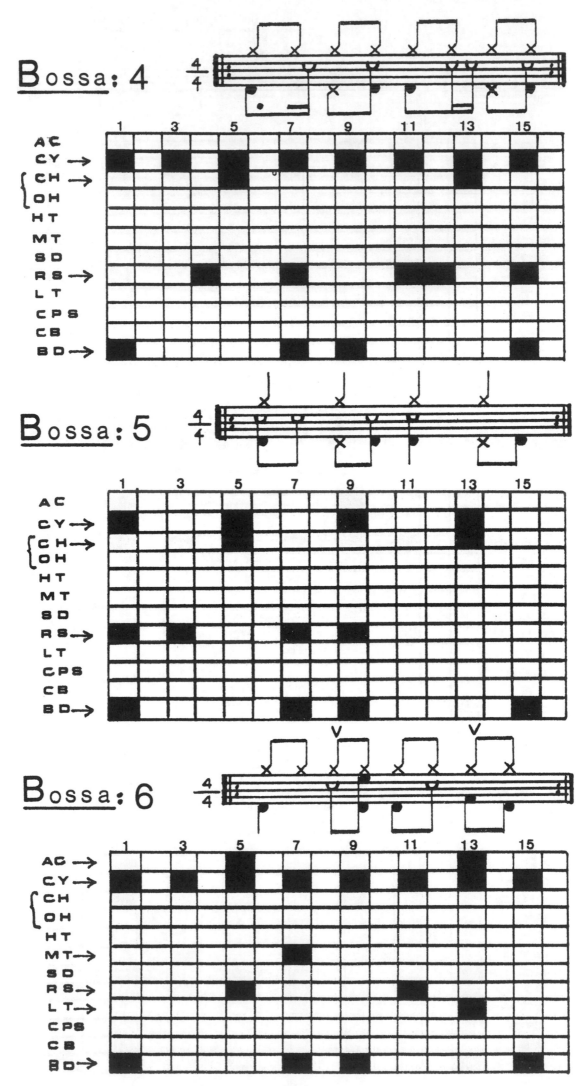

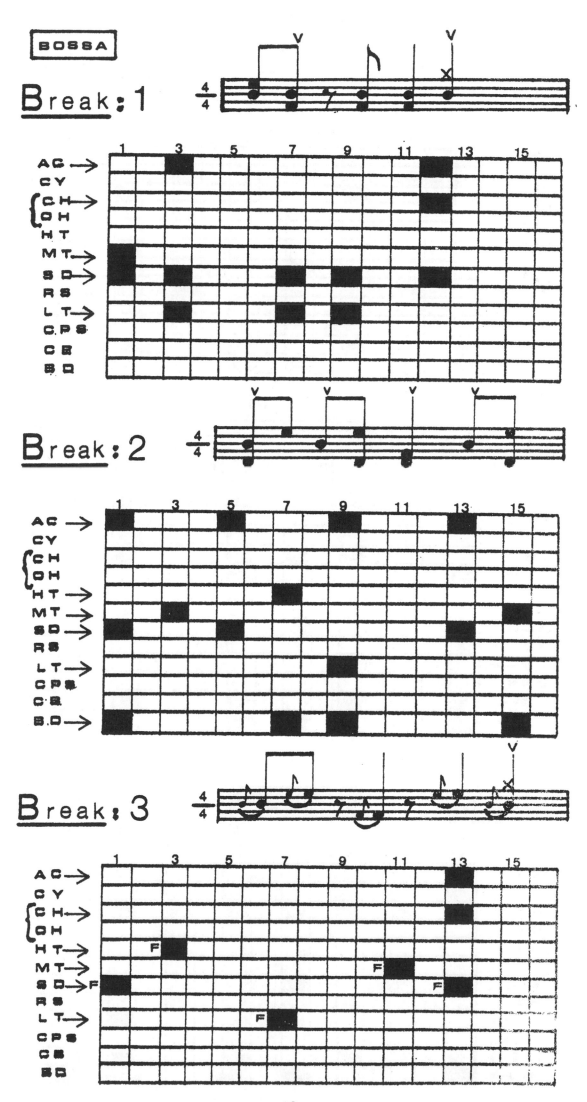

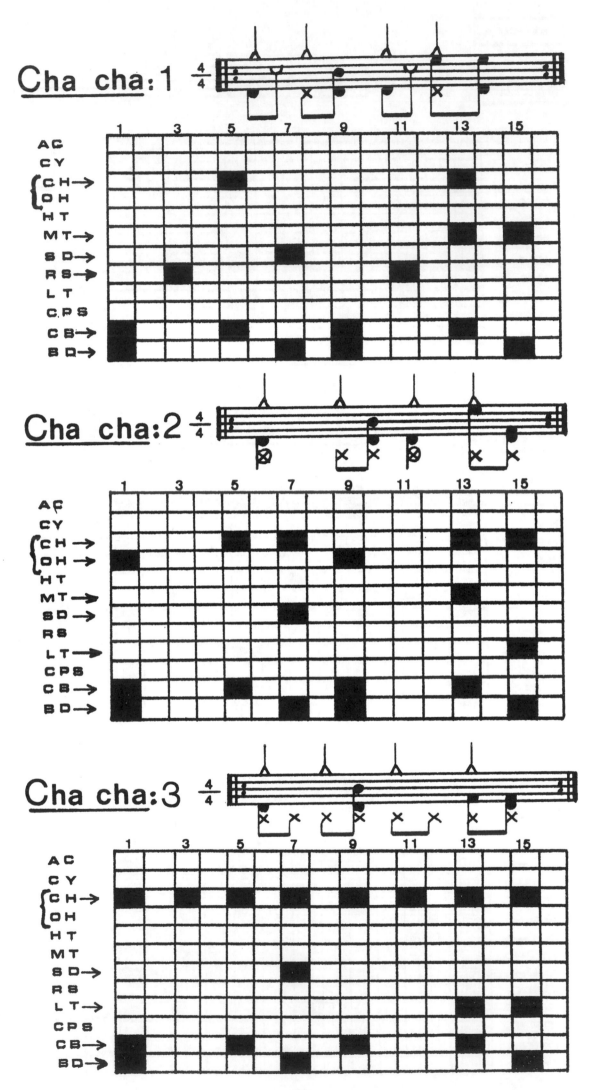

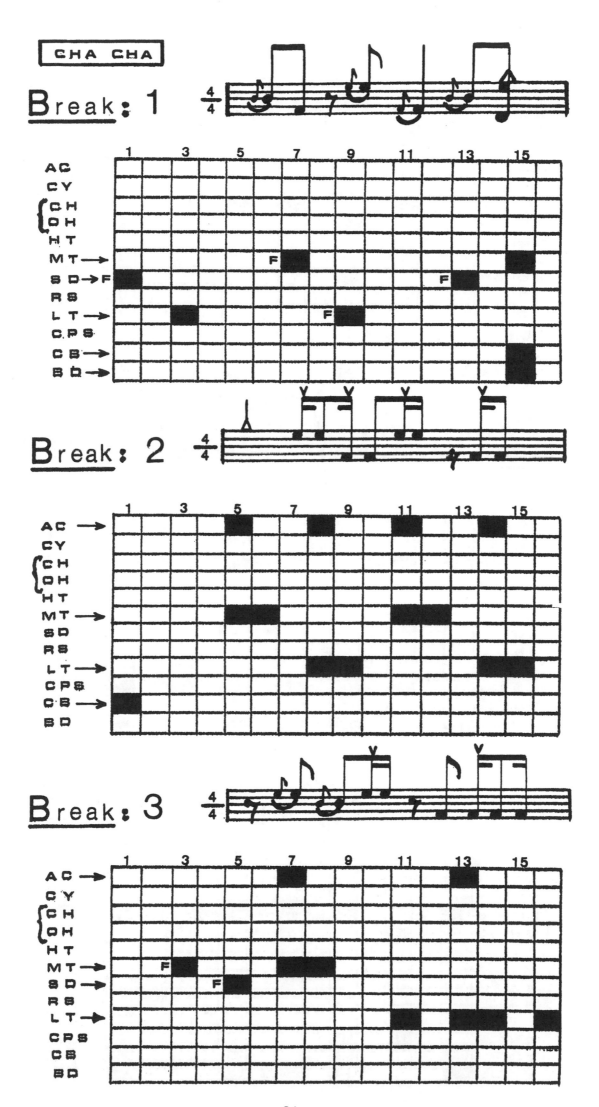

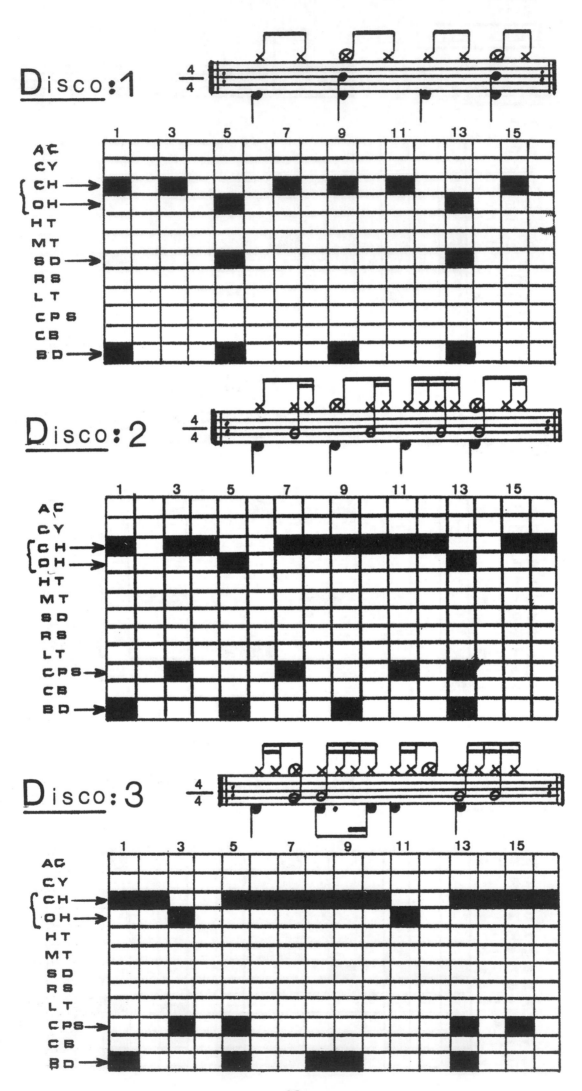

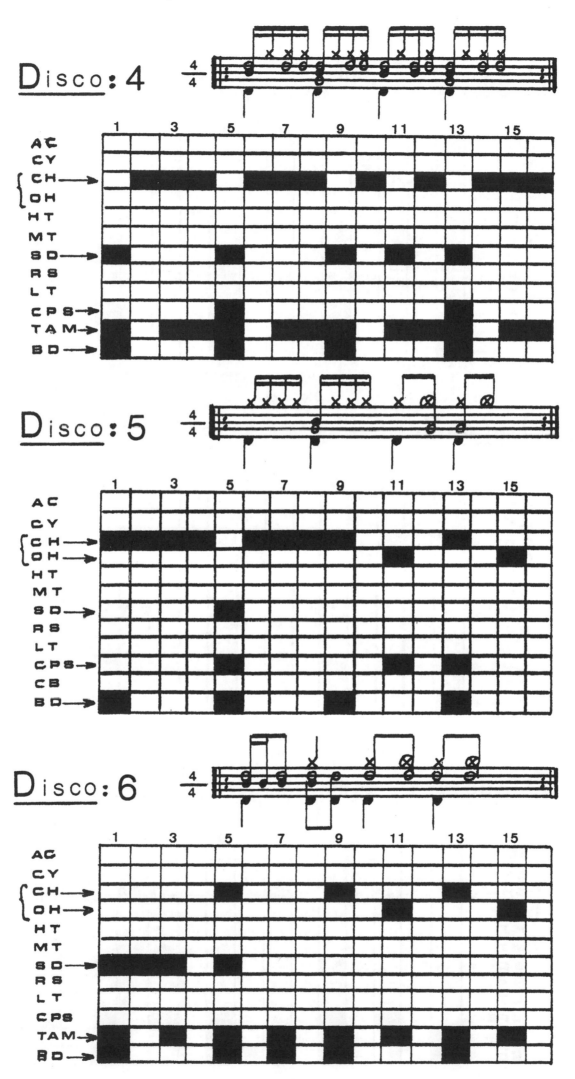

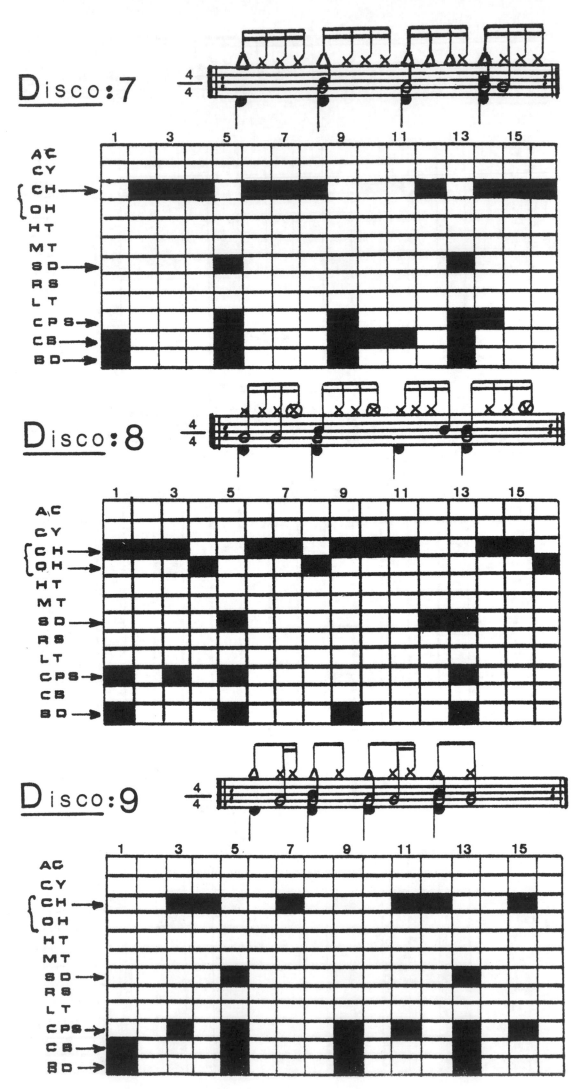

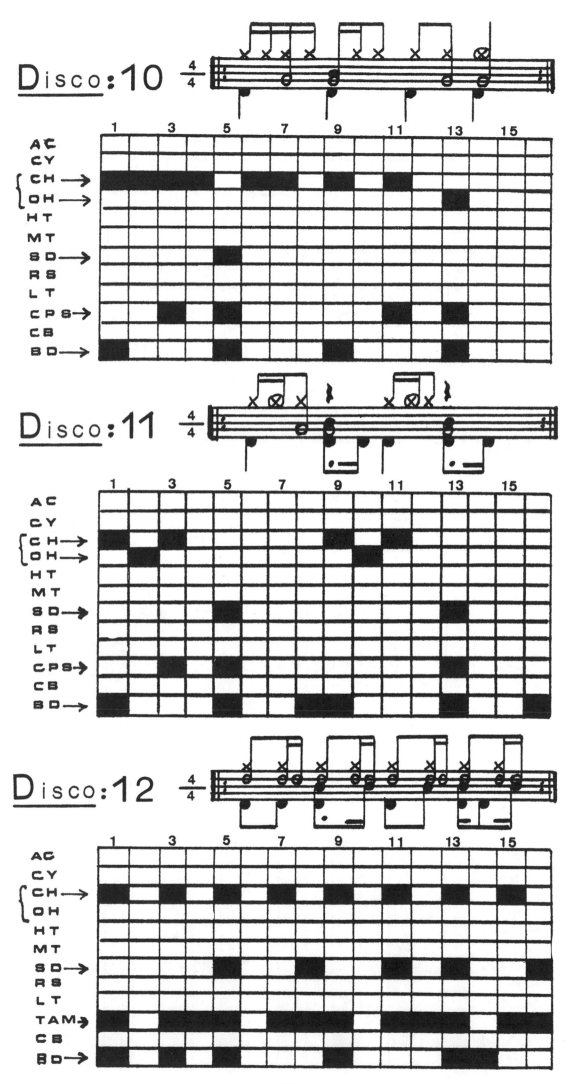

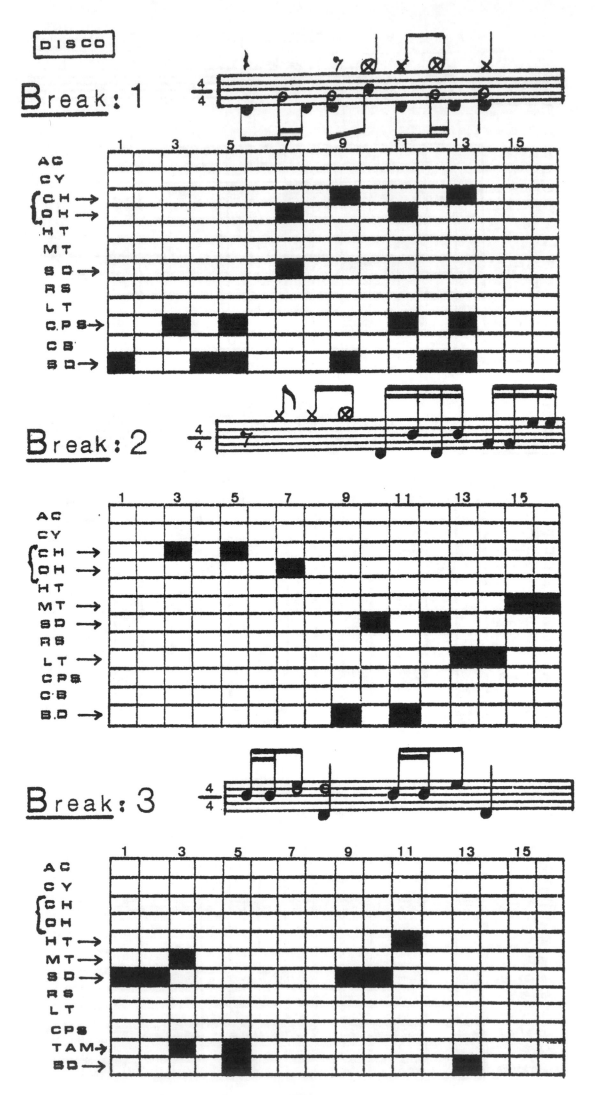

26

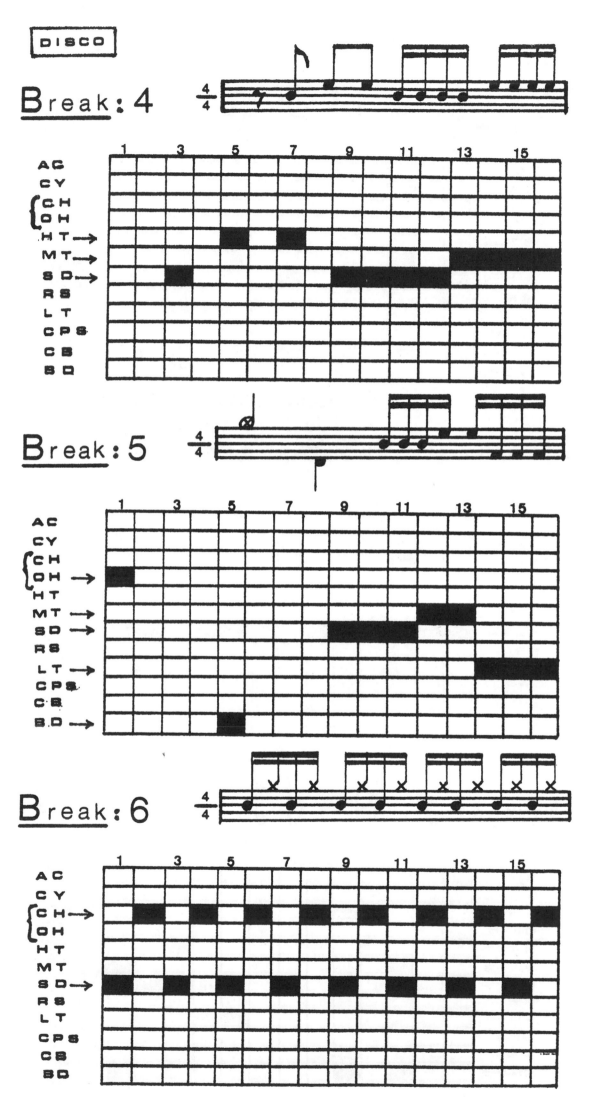

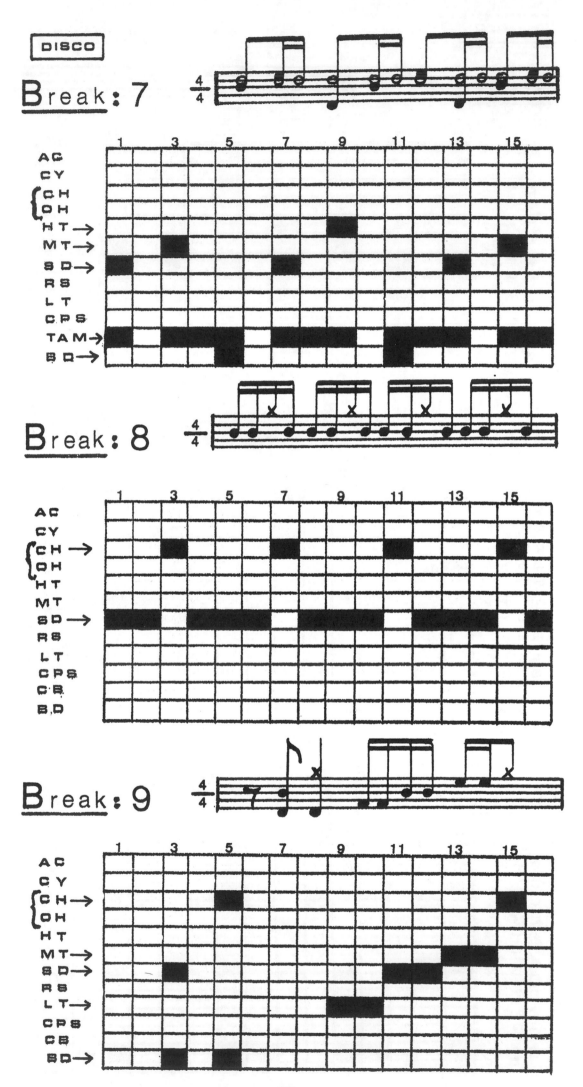

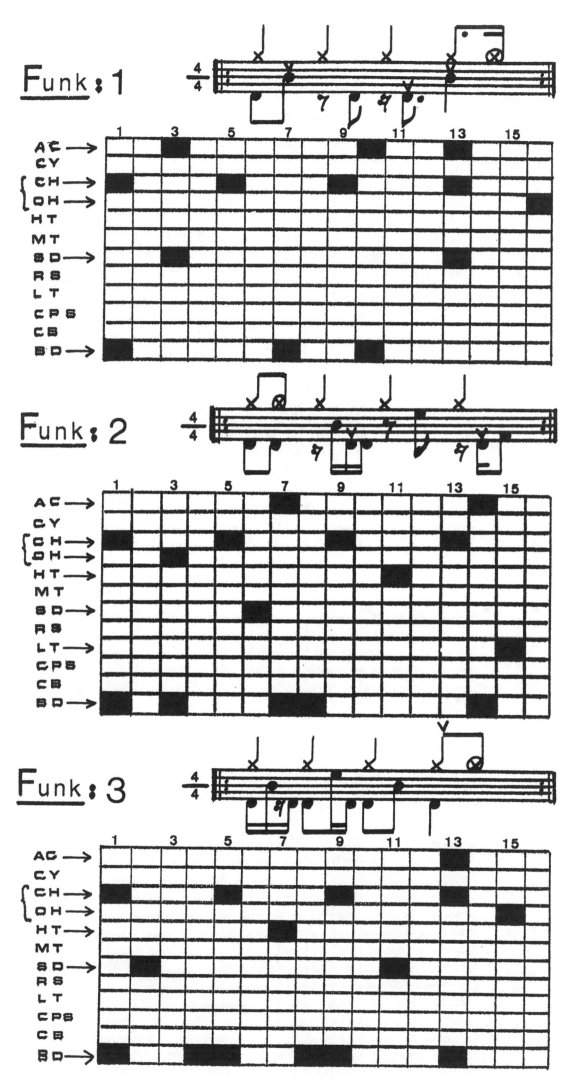

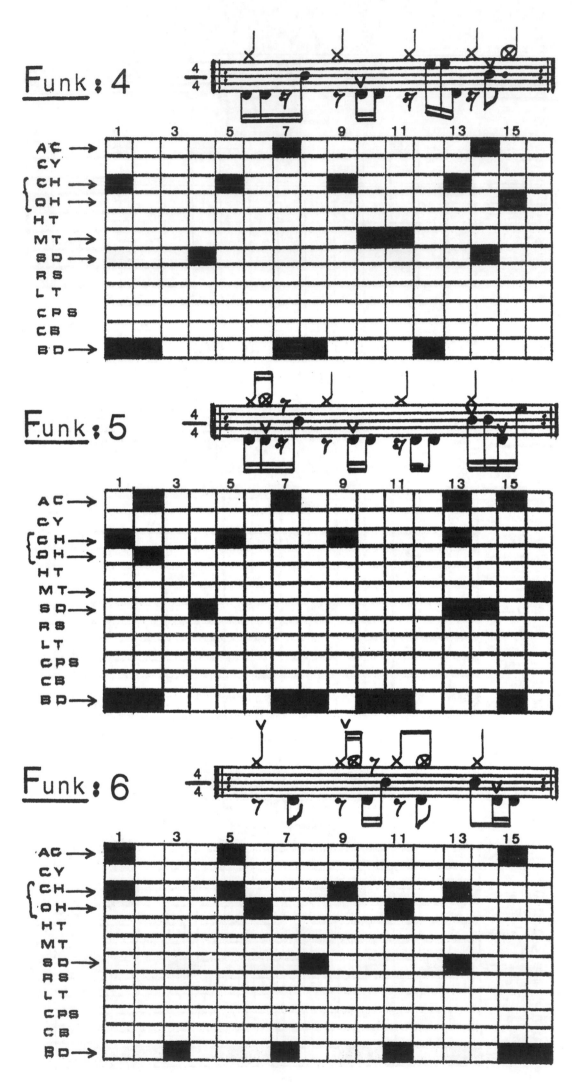

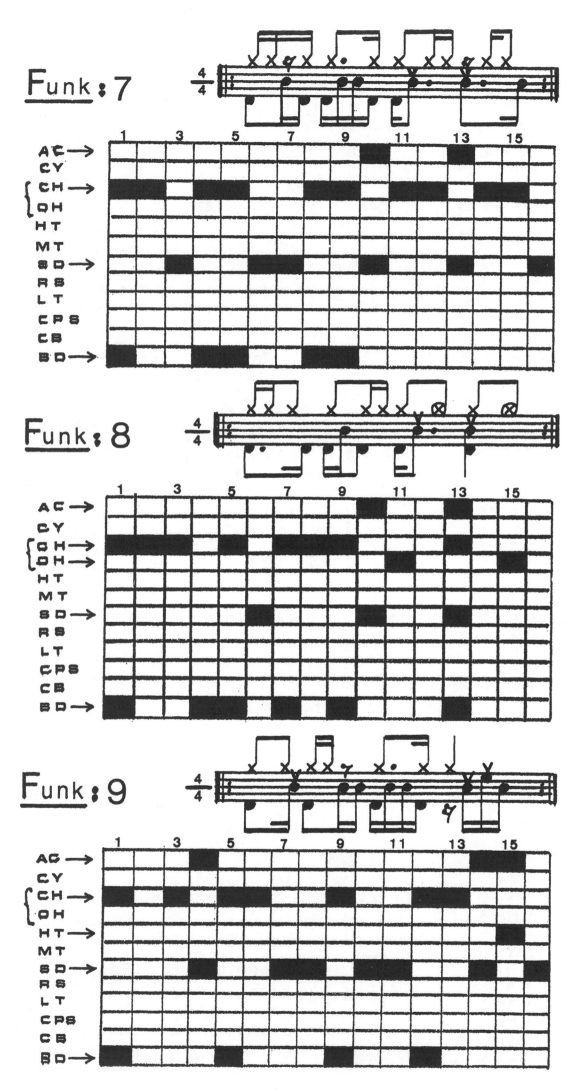

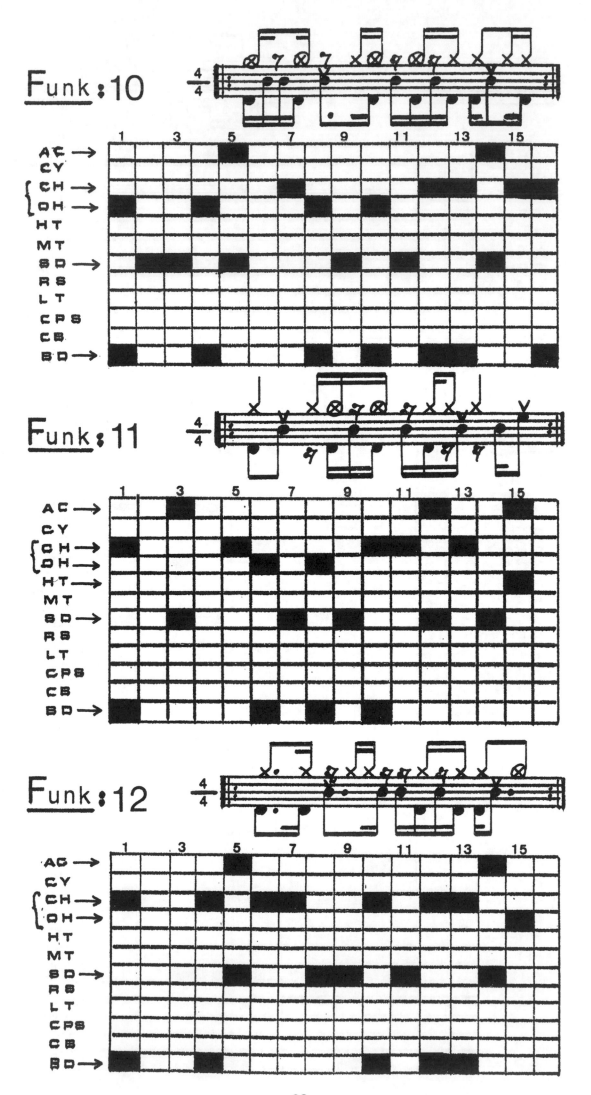

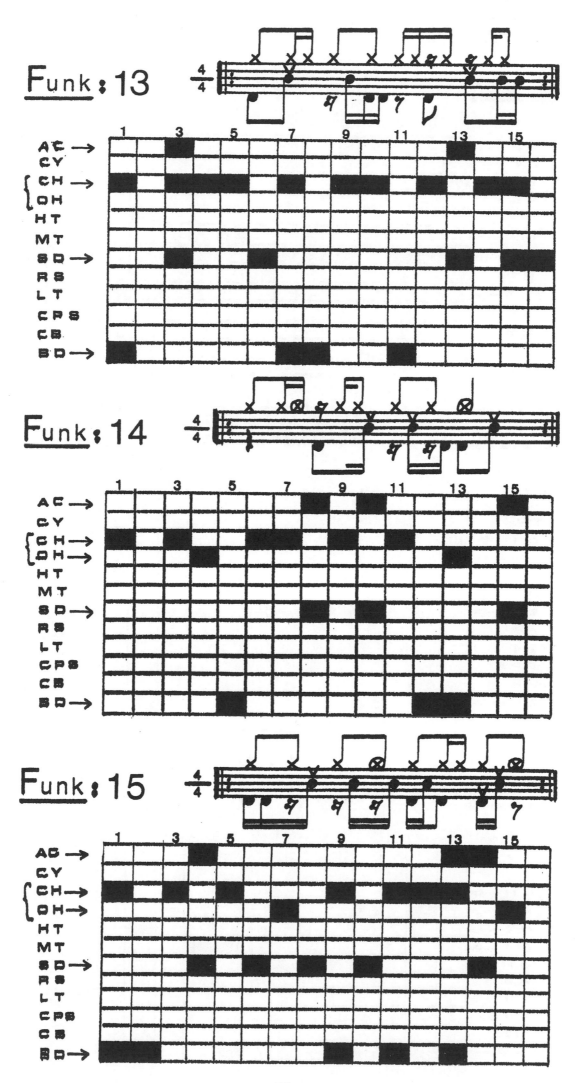

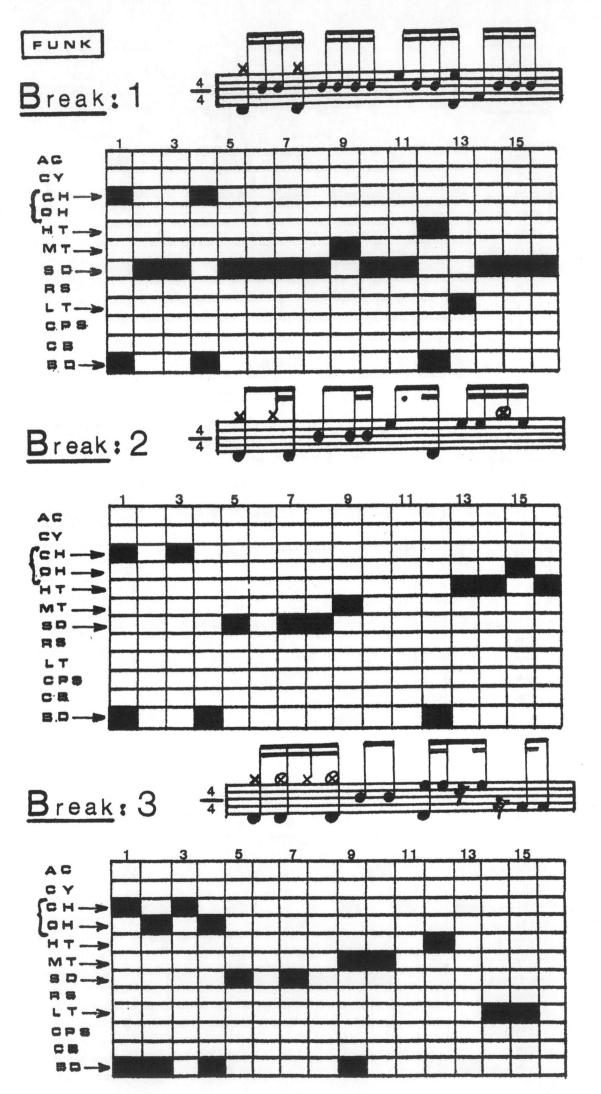

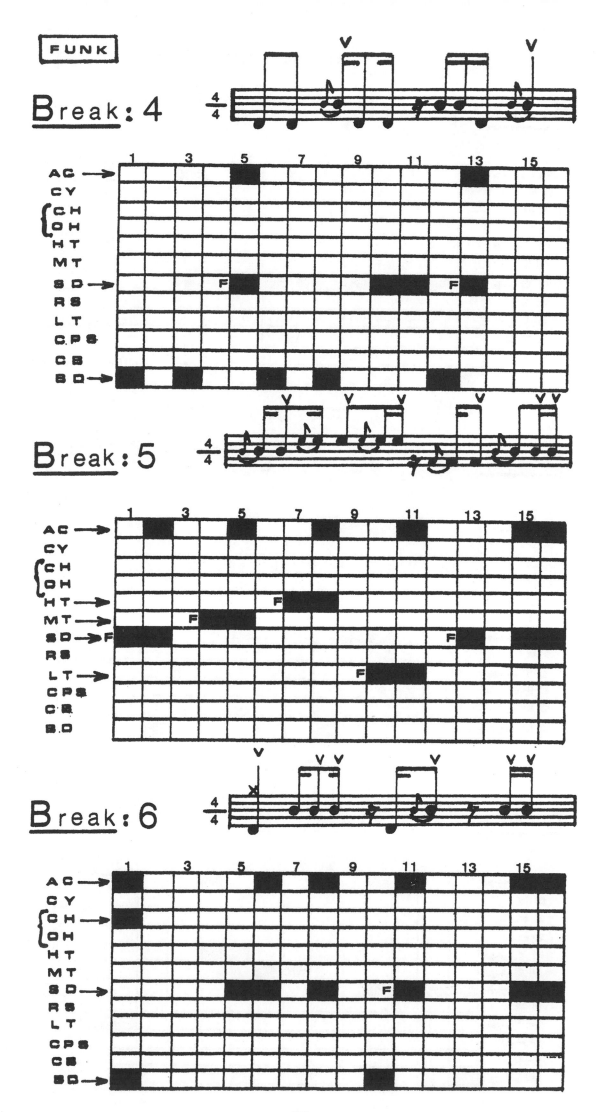

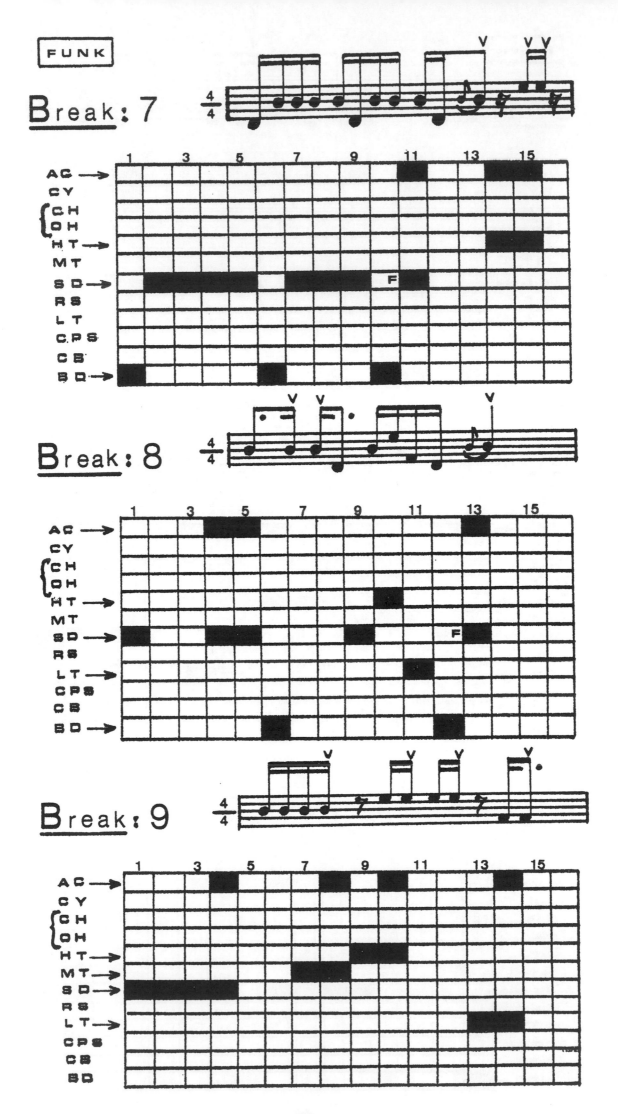

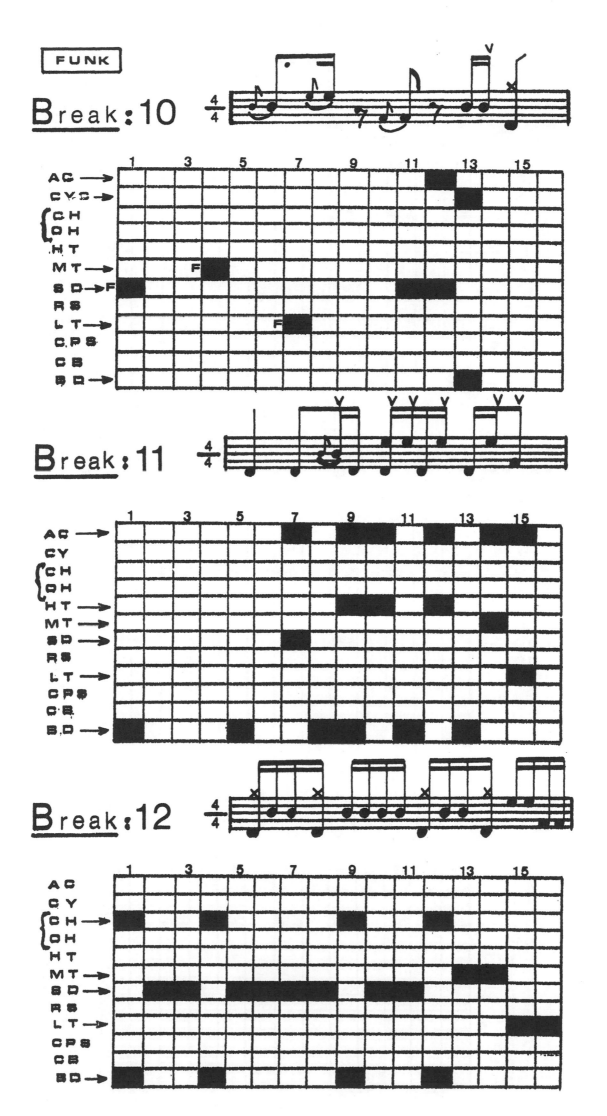

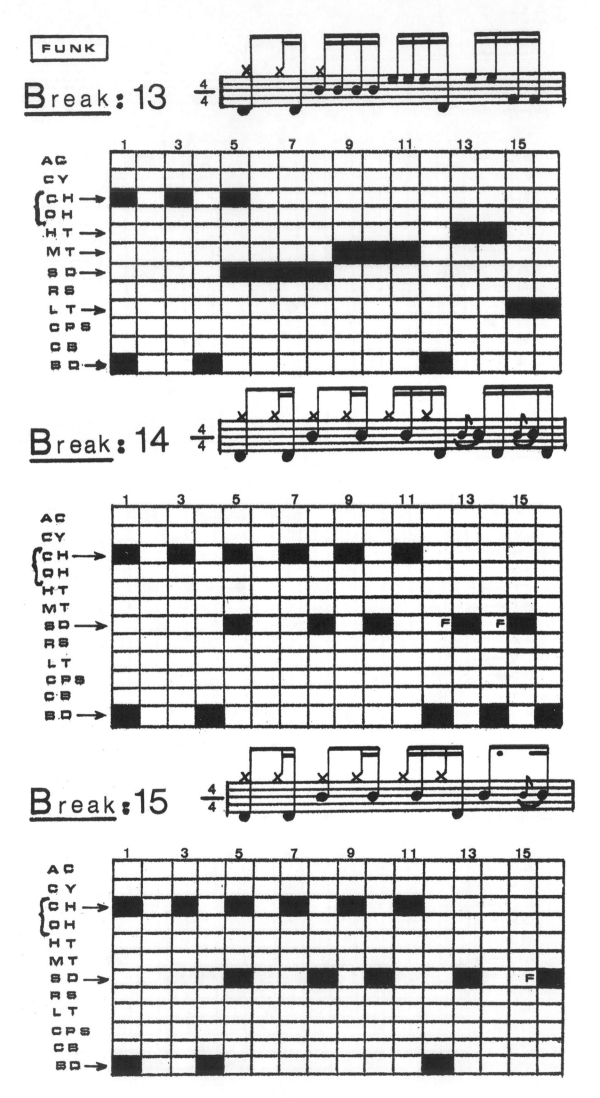

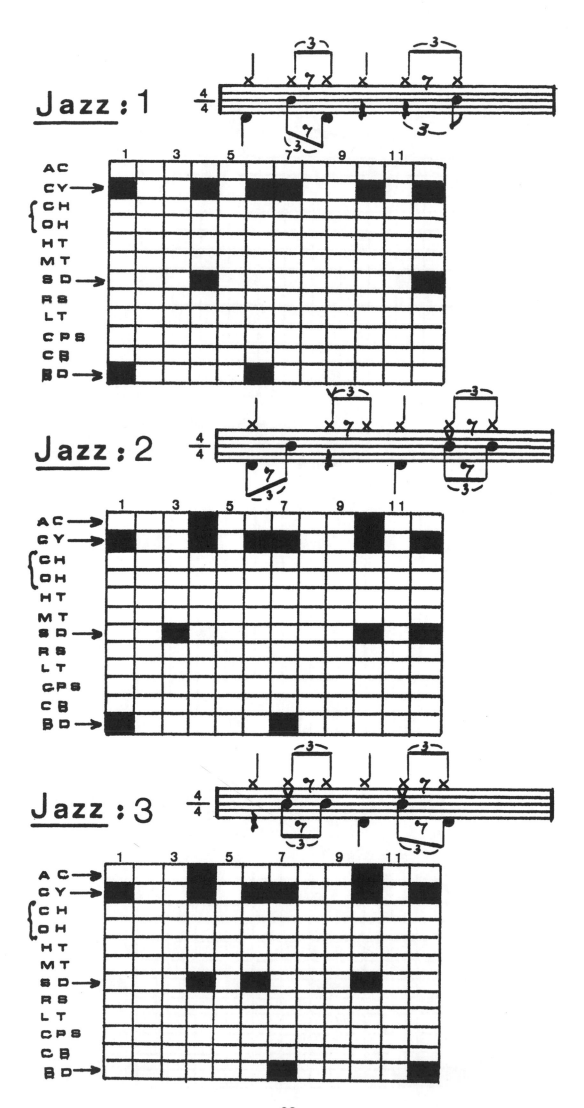

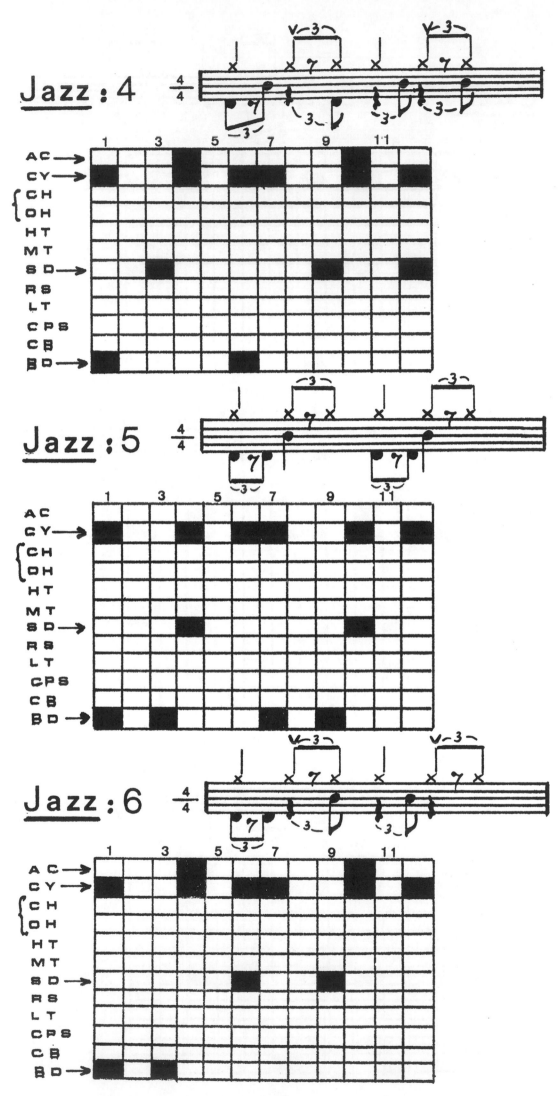

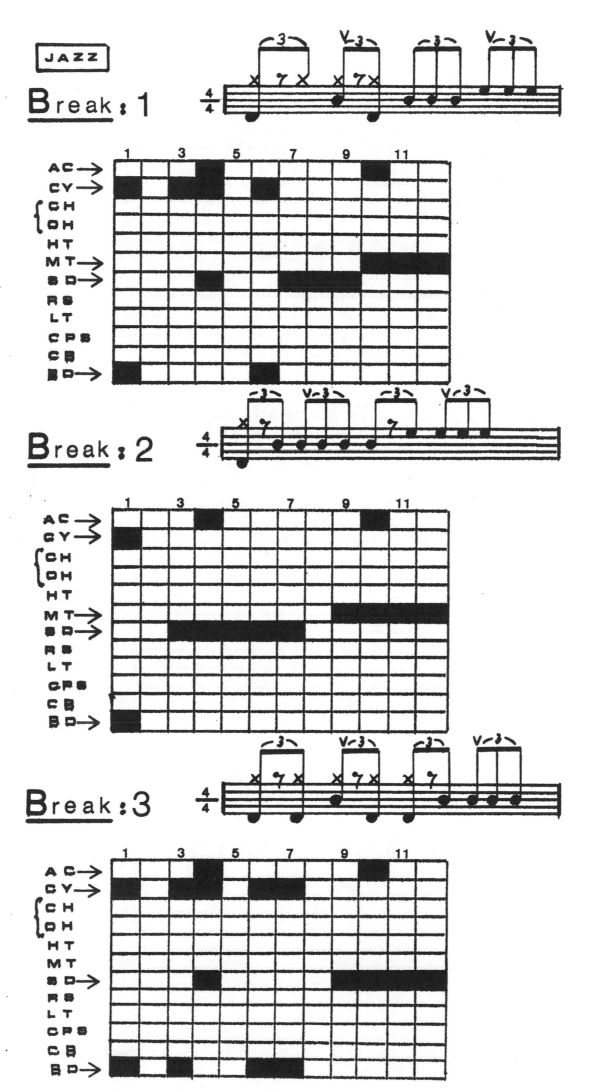

March:1

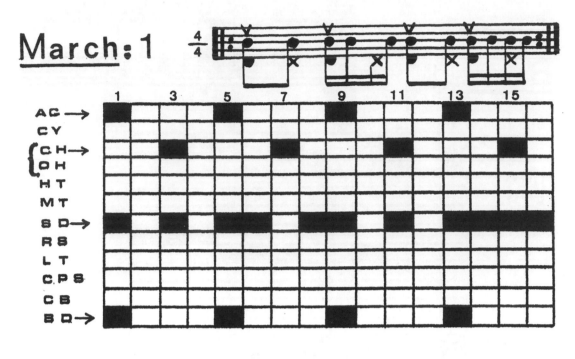

March:2

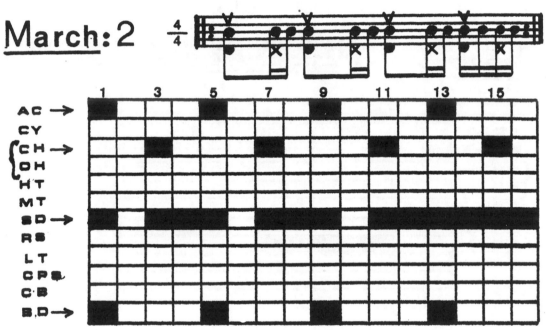

Tango:

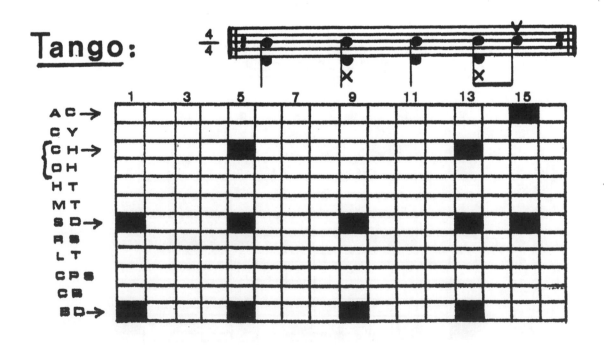

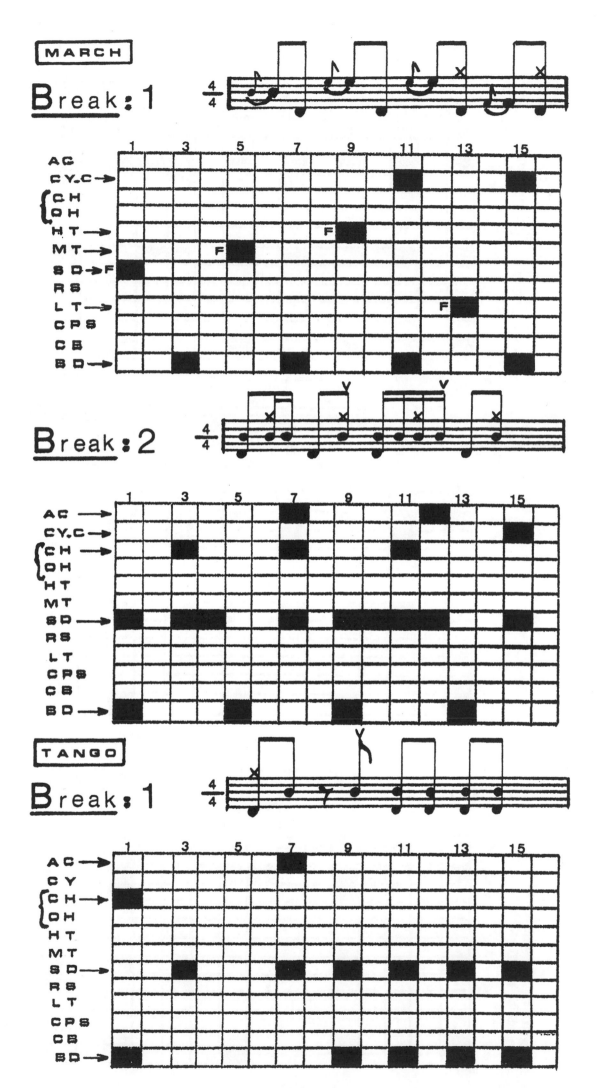

43

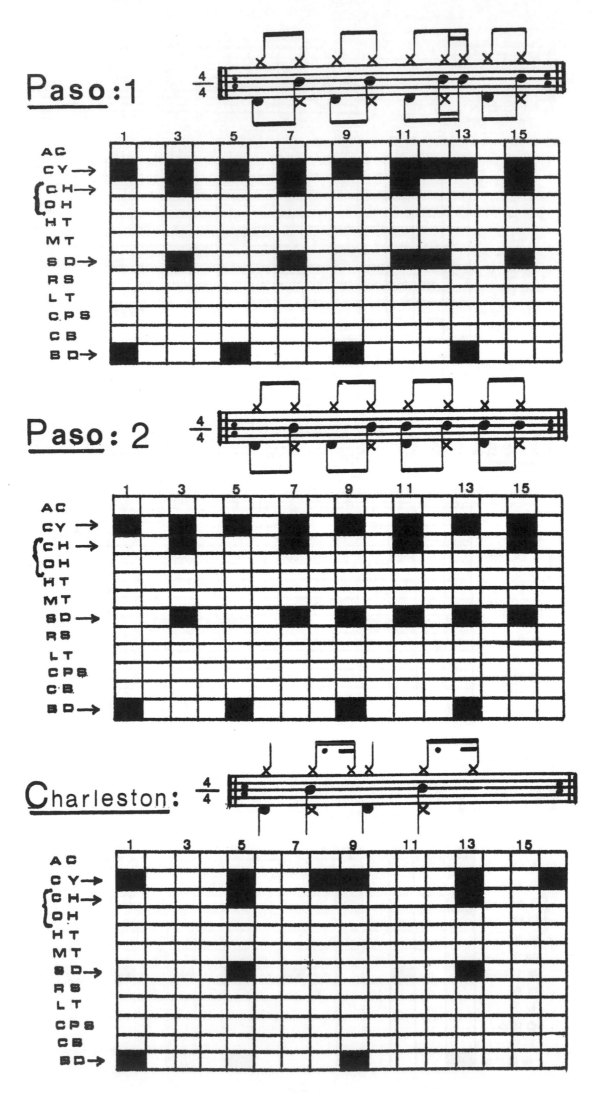

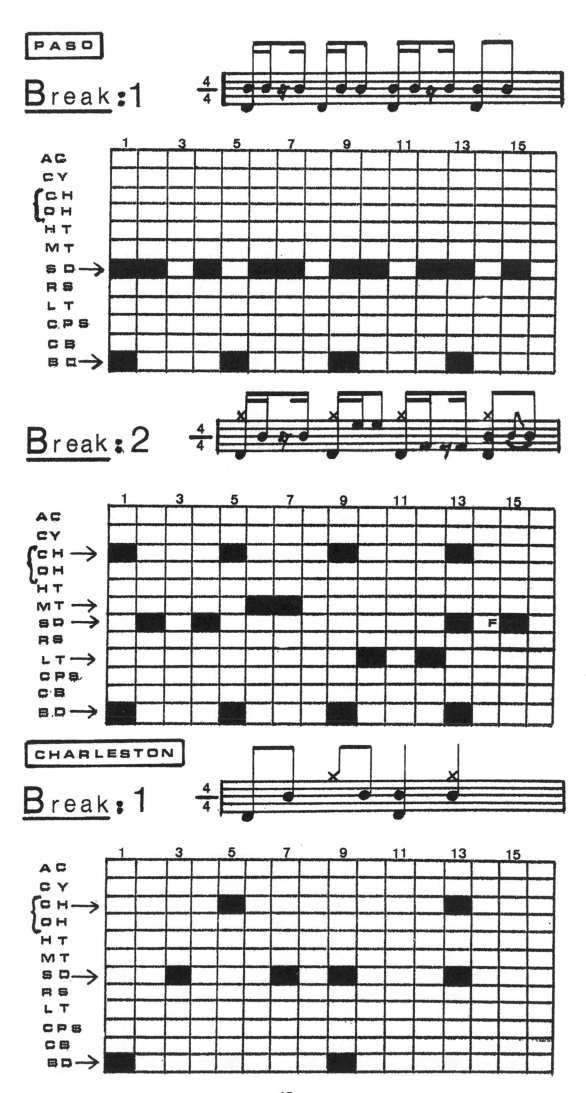

45

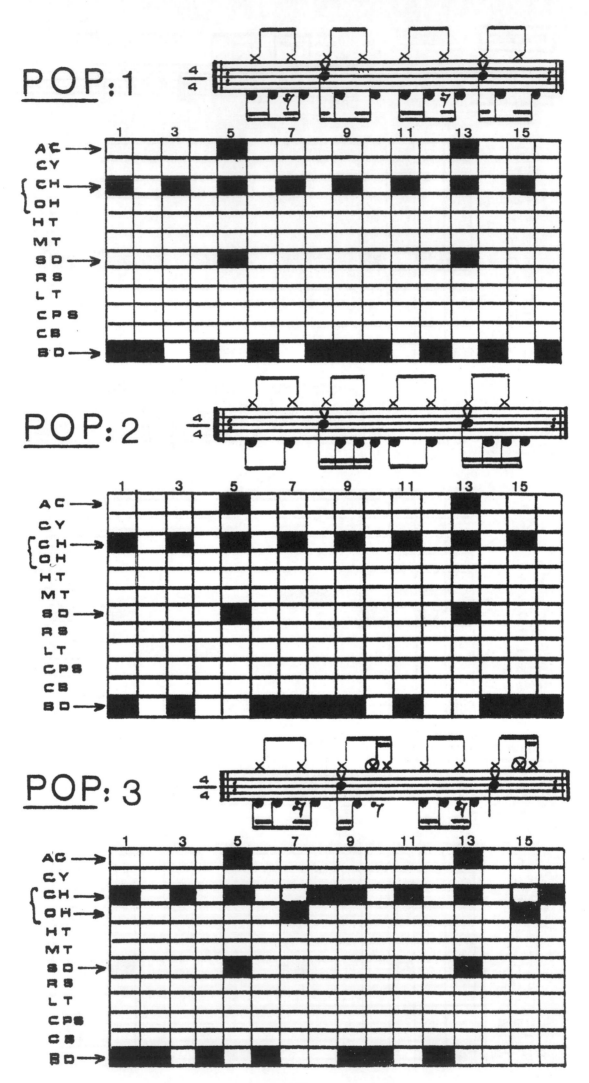

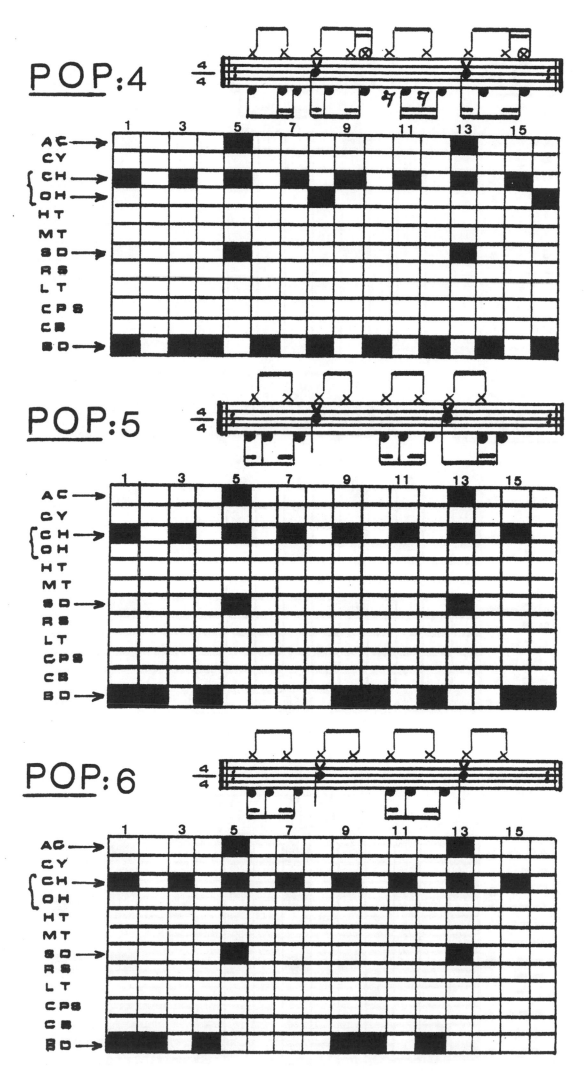

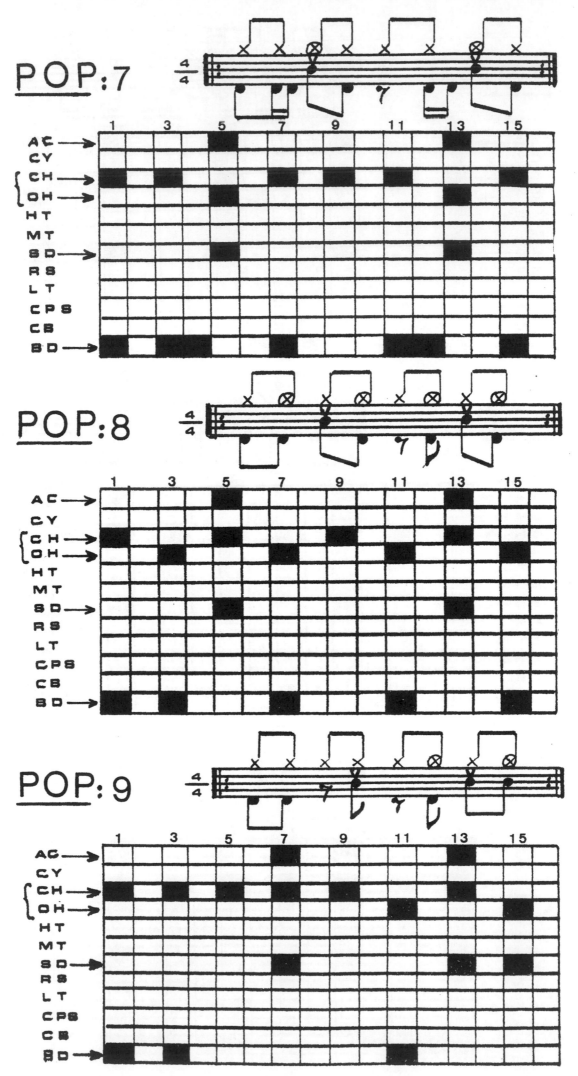

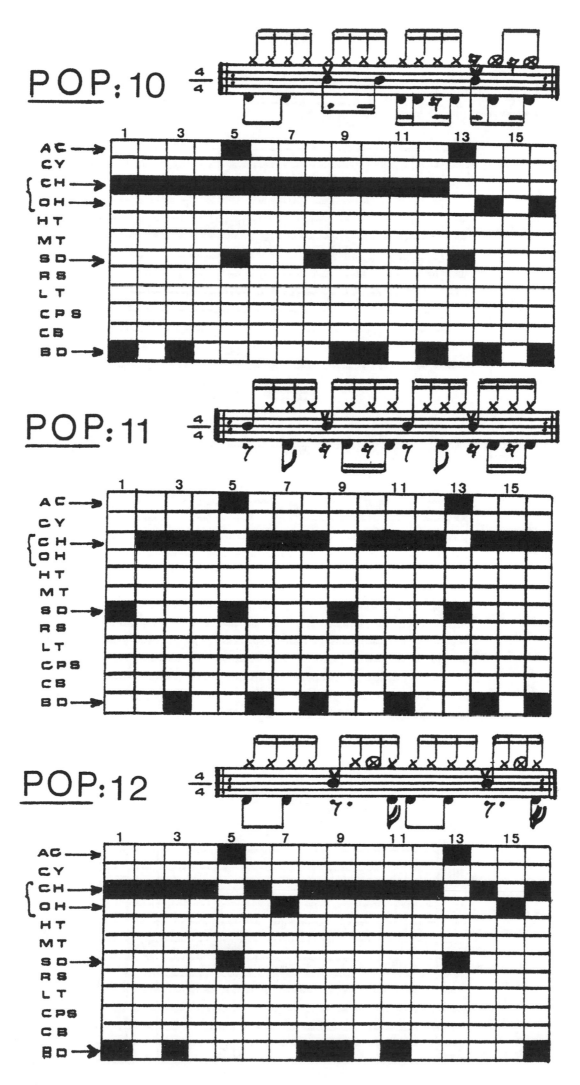

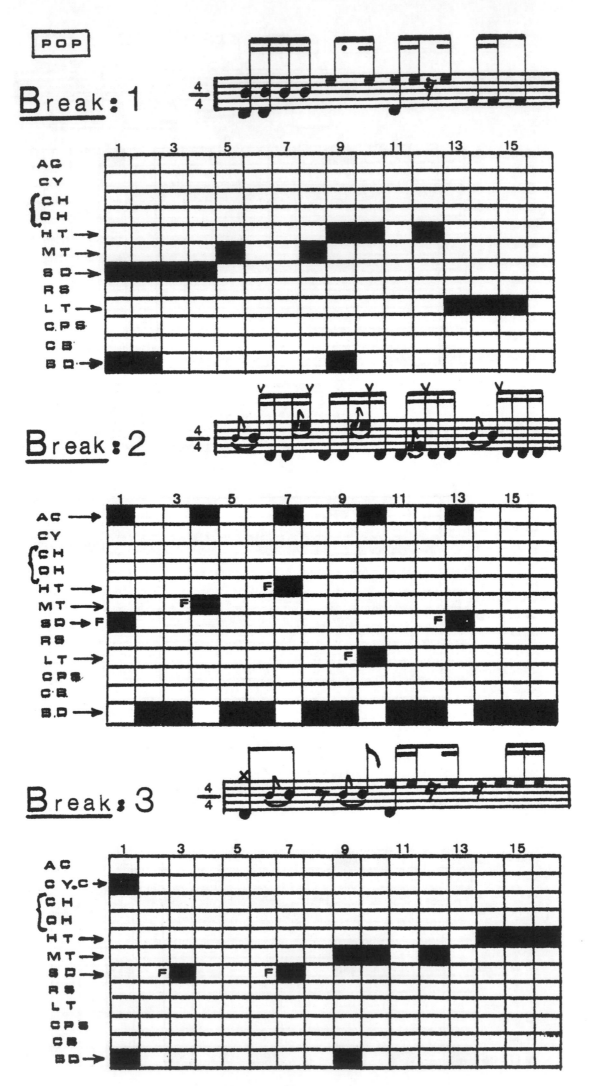

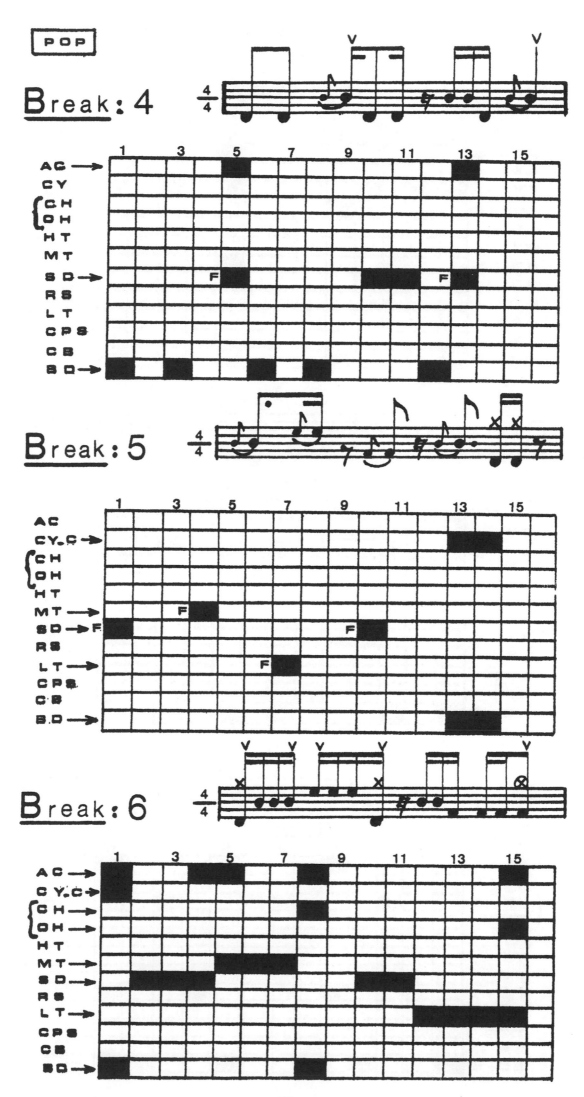

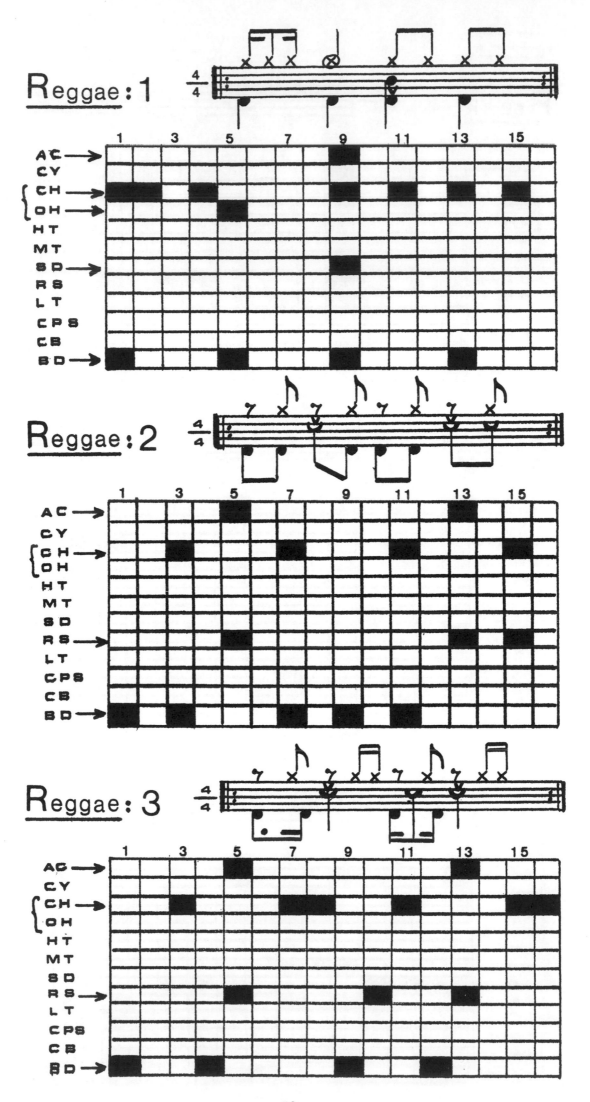

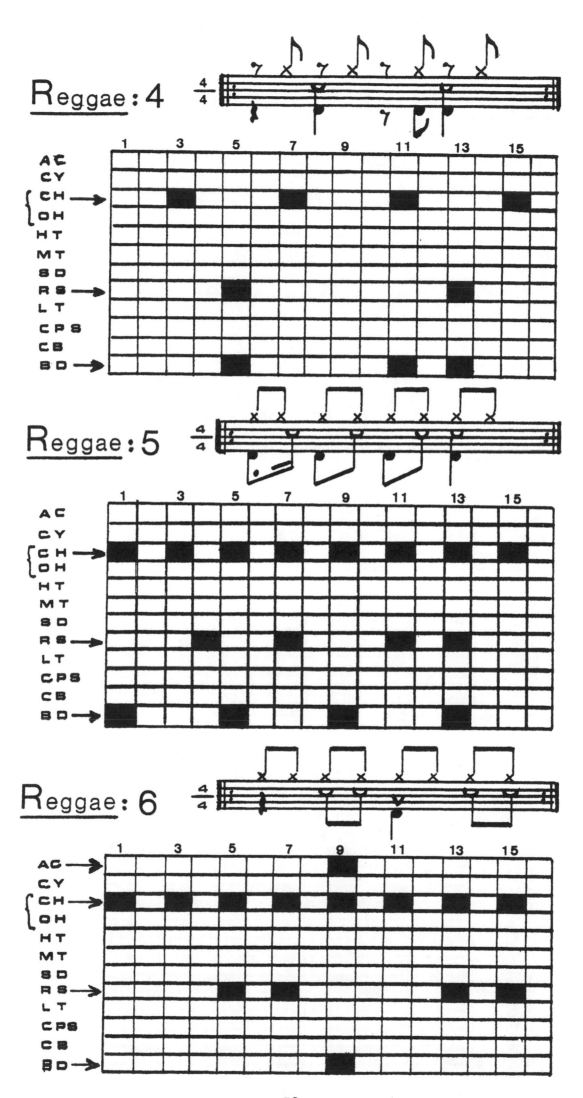

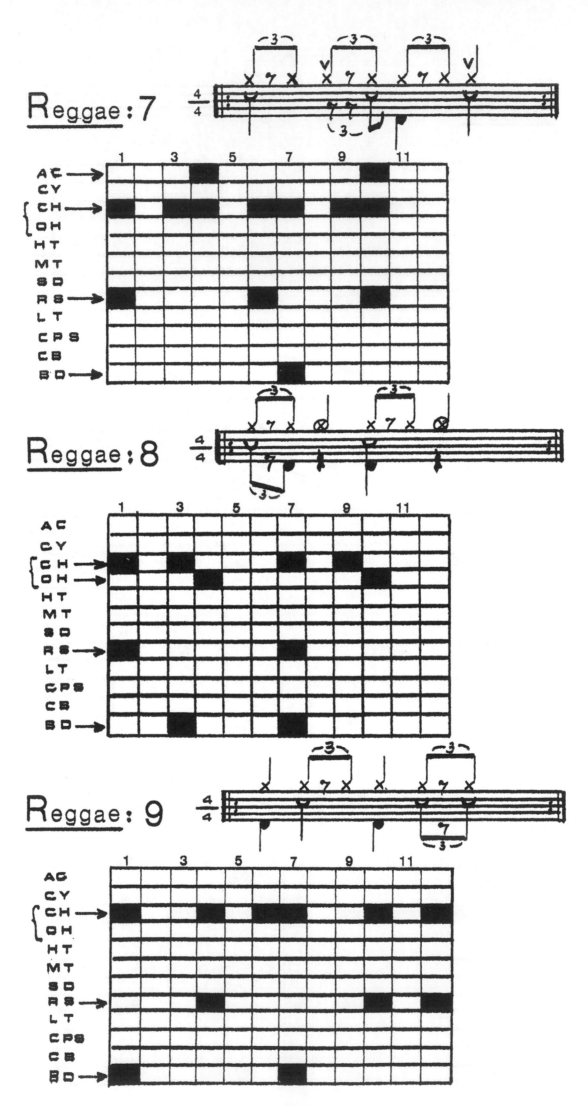

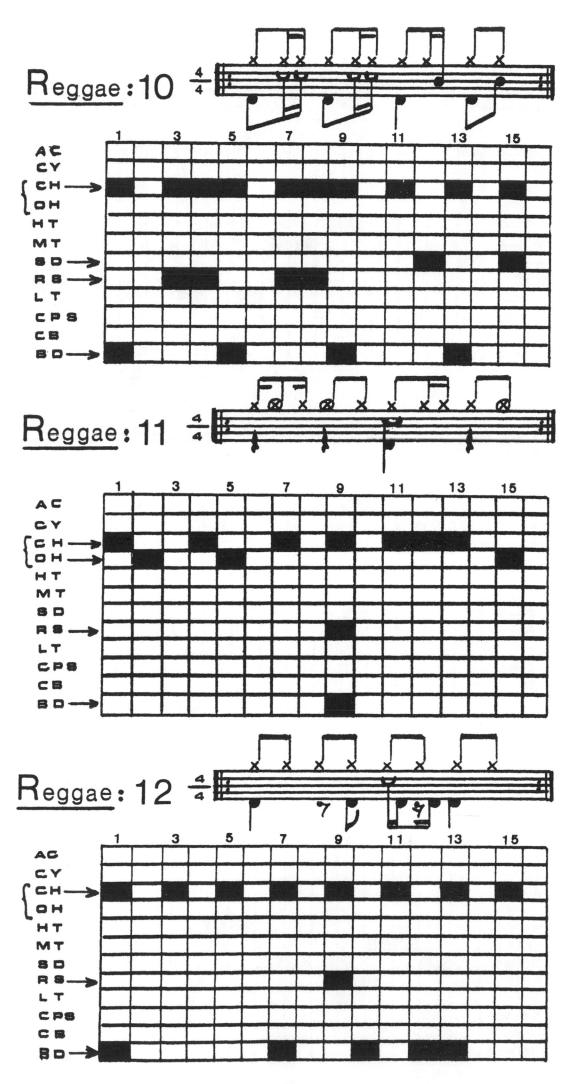

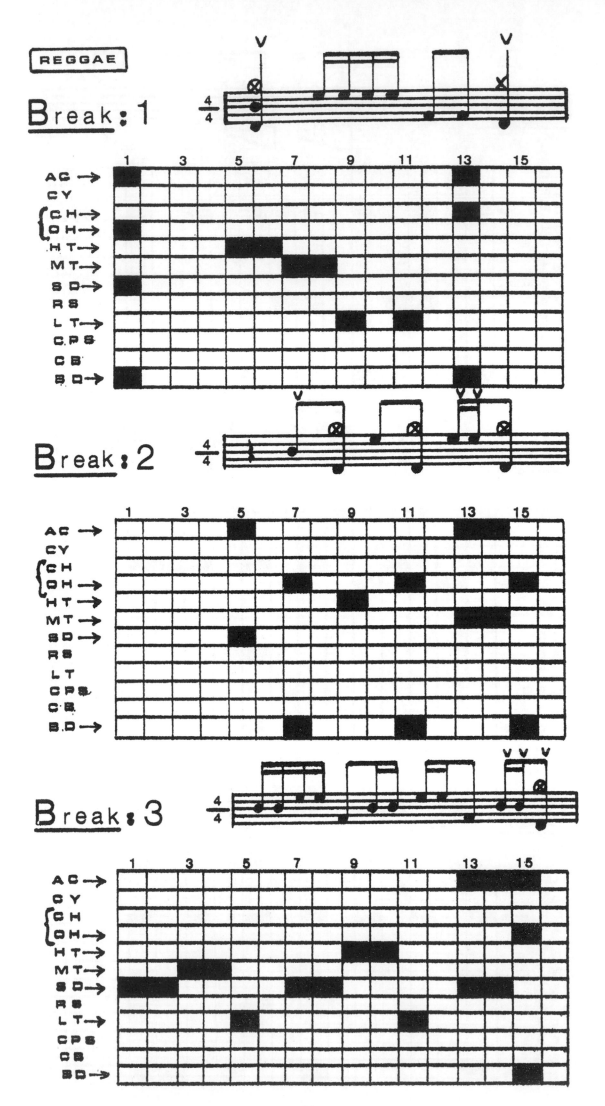

REGGAE

Break: 1

Break: 2

Break: 3

56

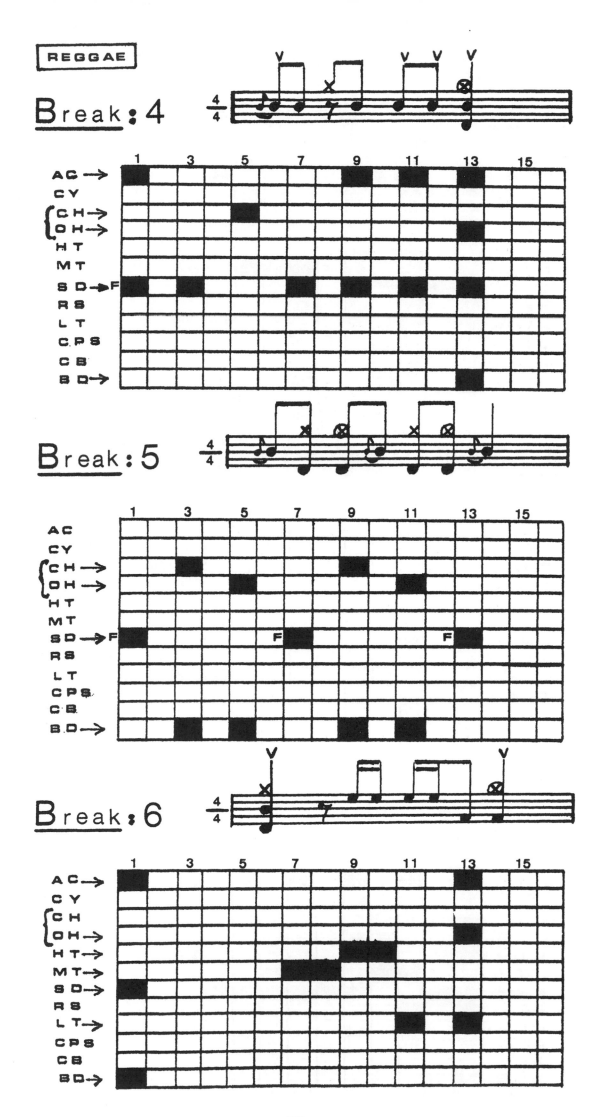

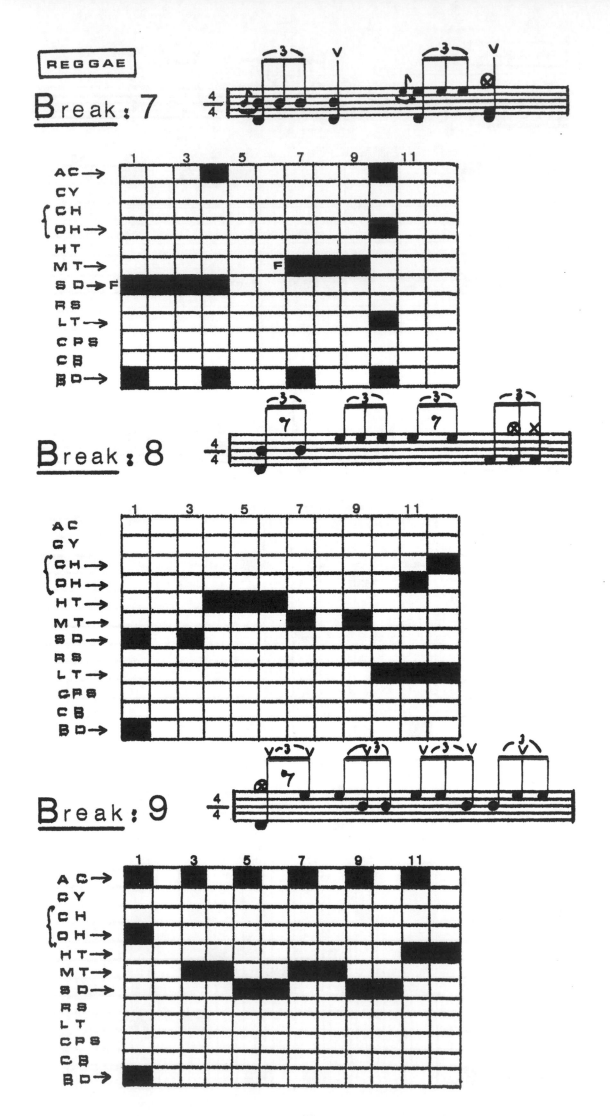

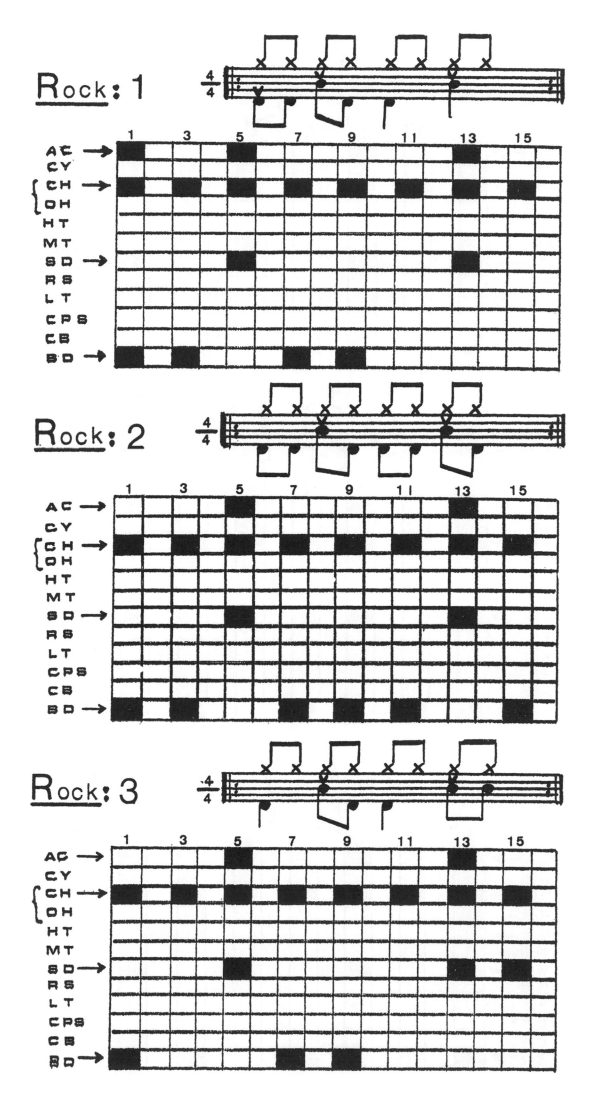

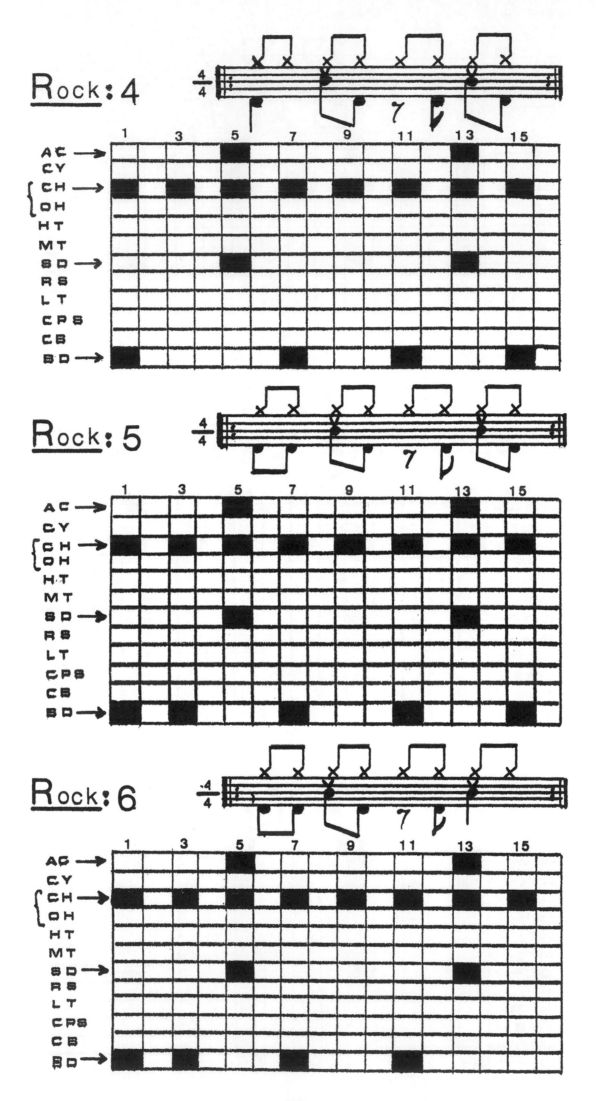

60

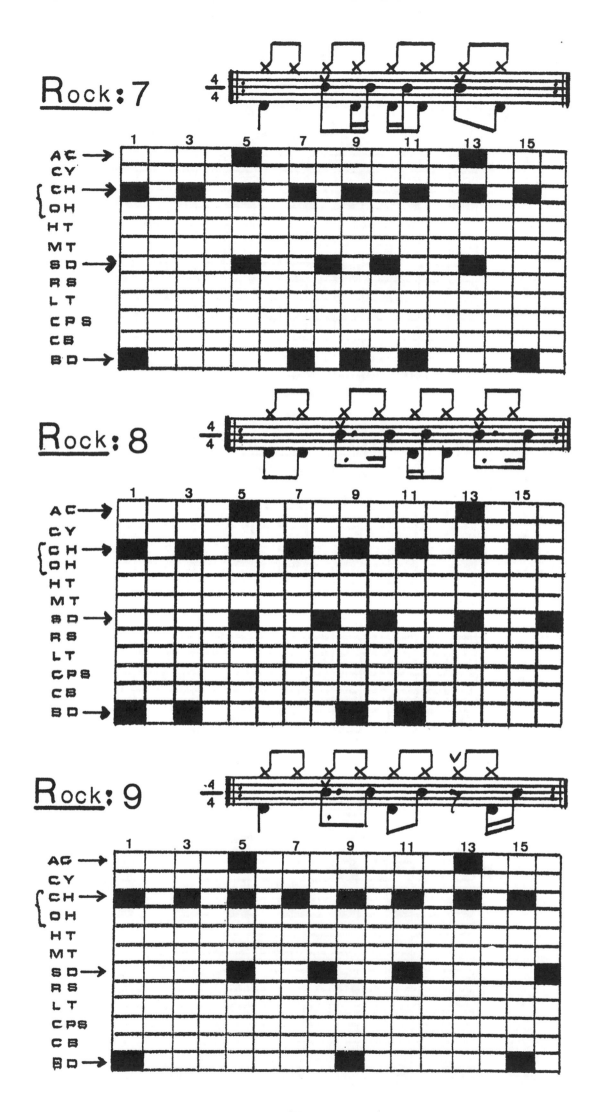

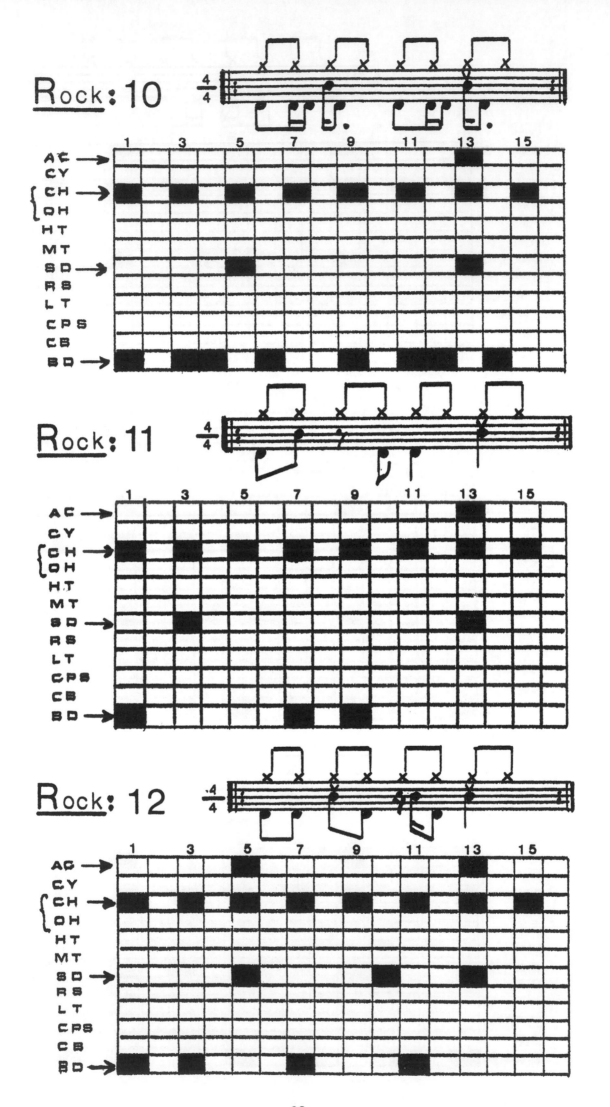

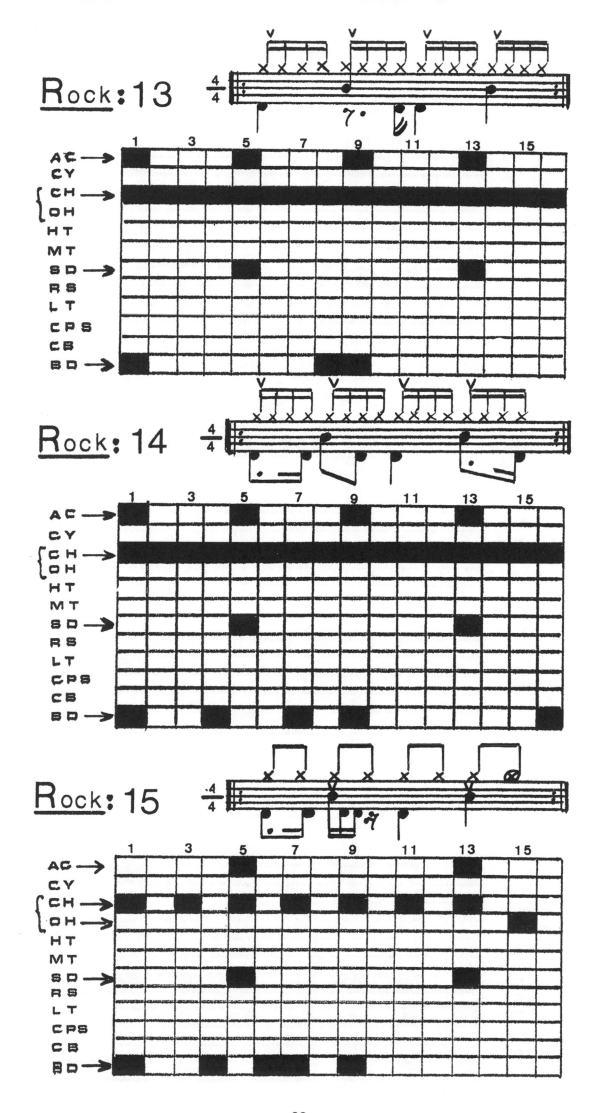

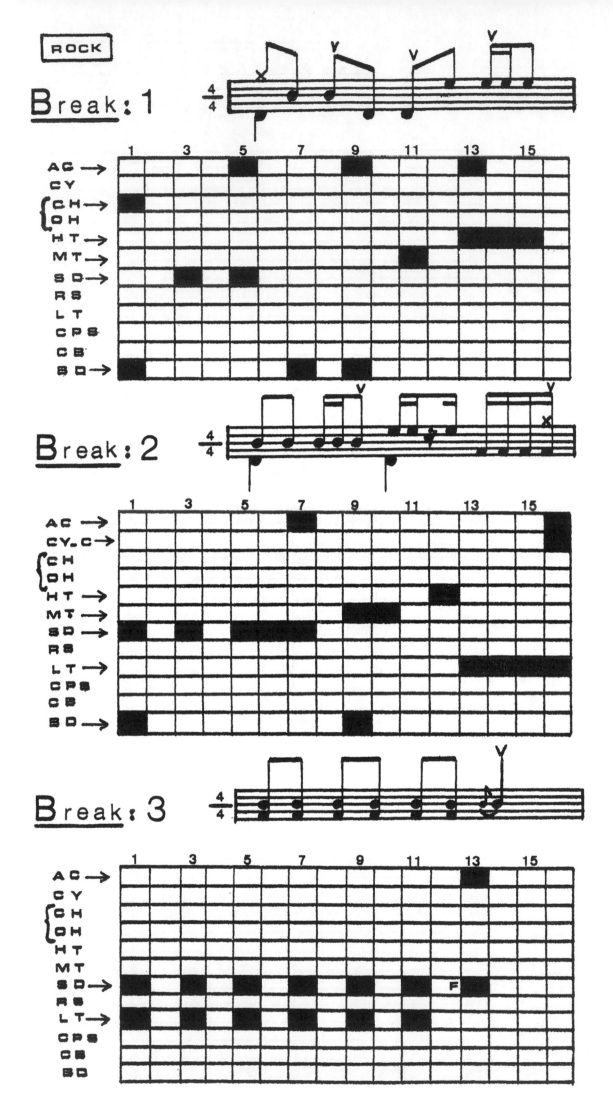

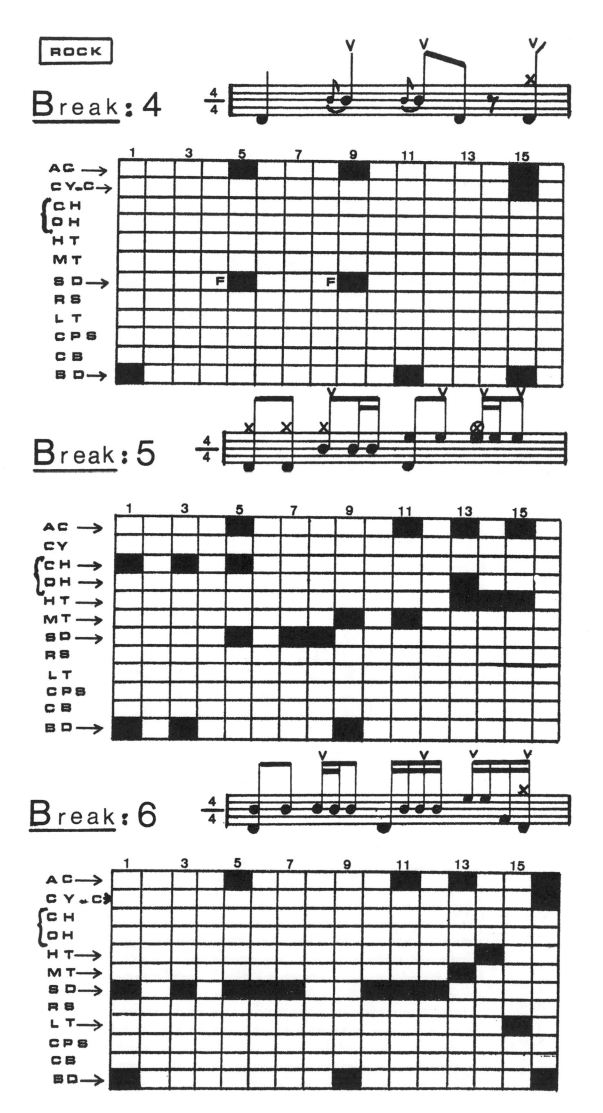

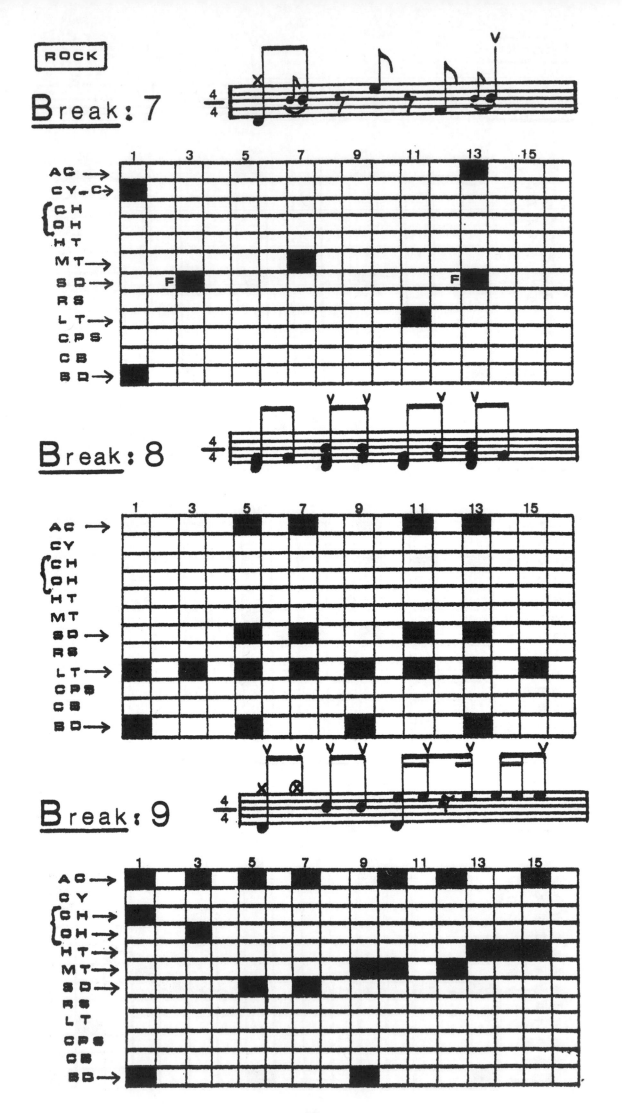

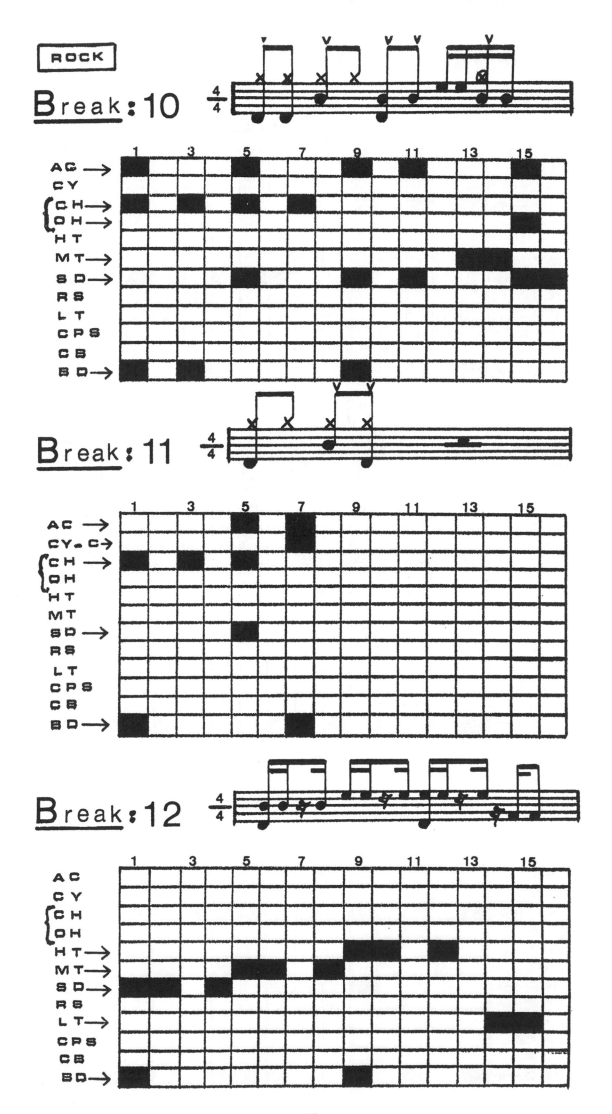

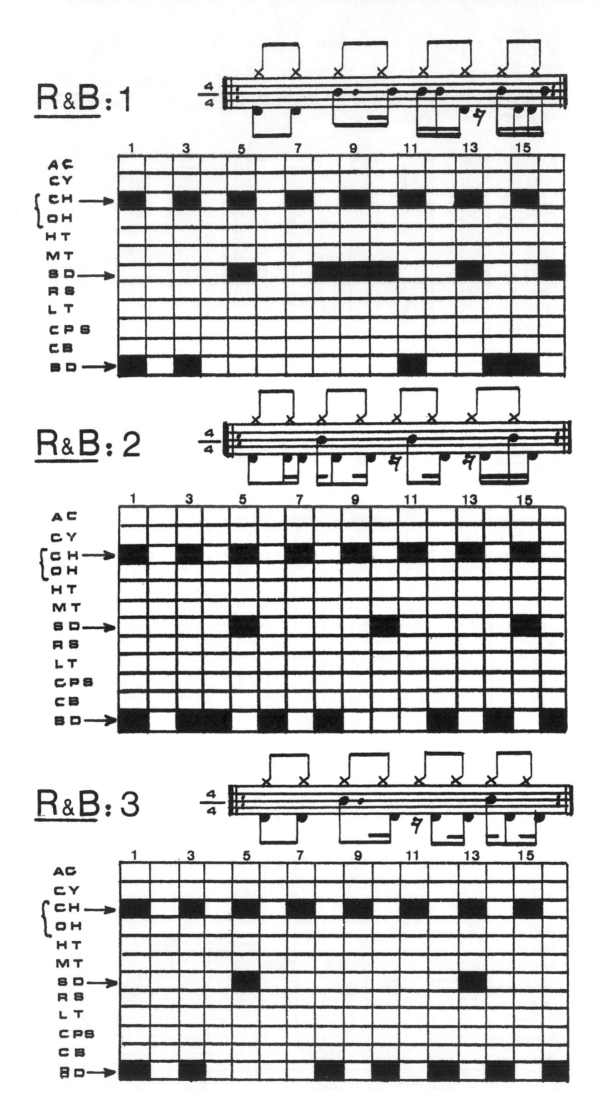

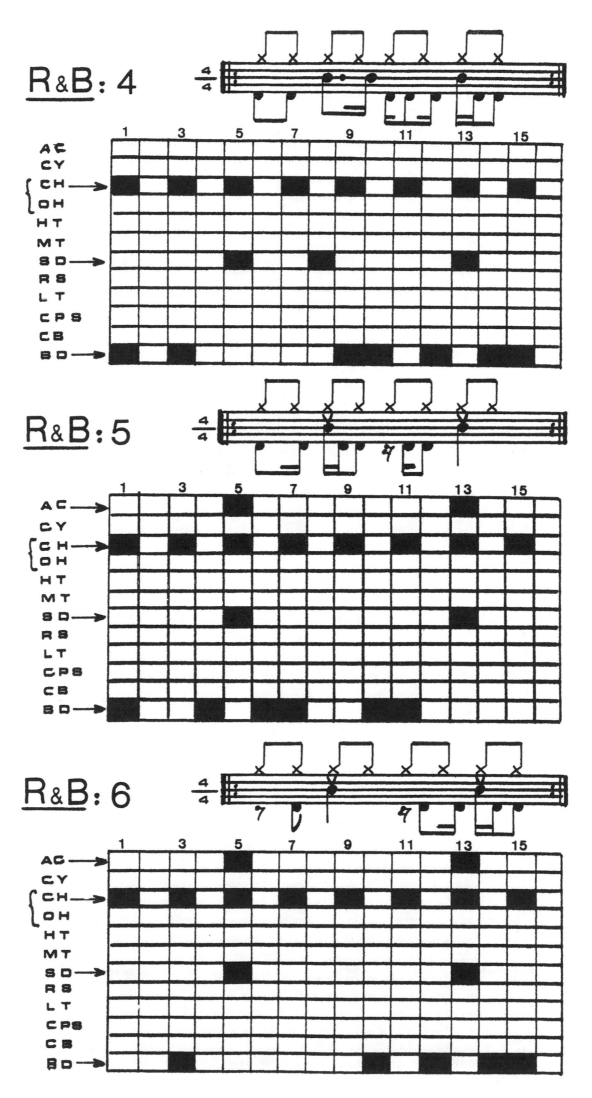

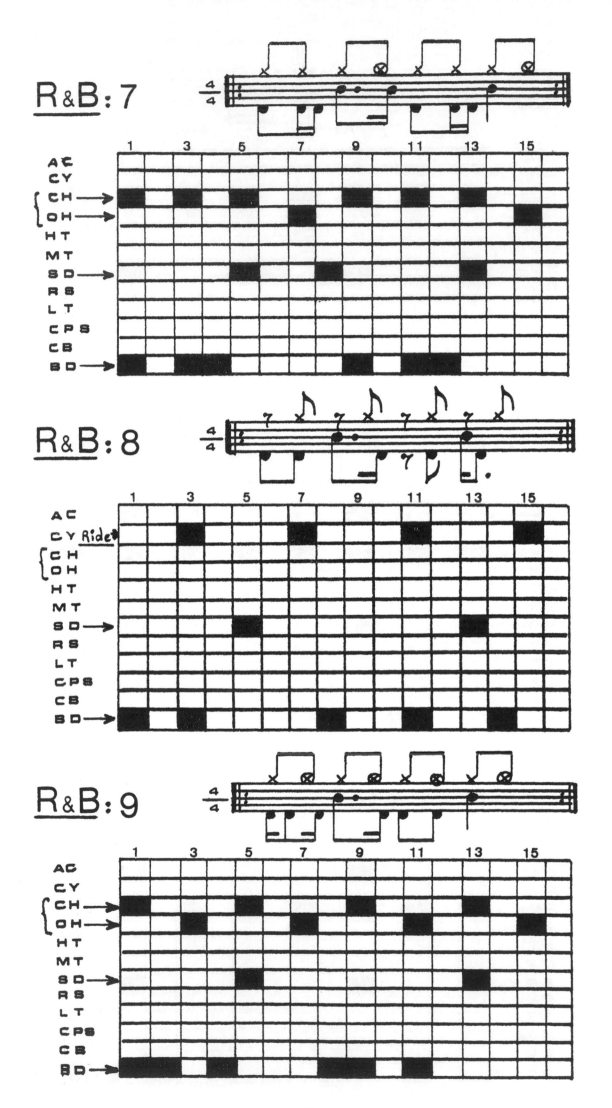

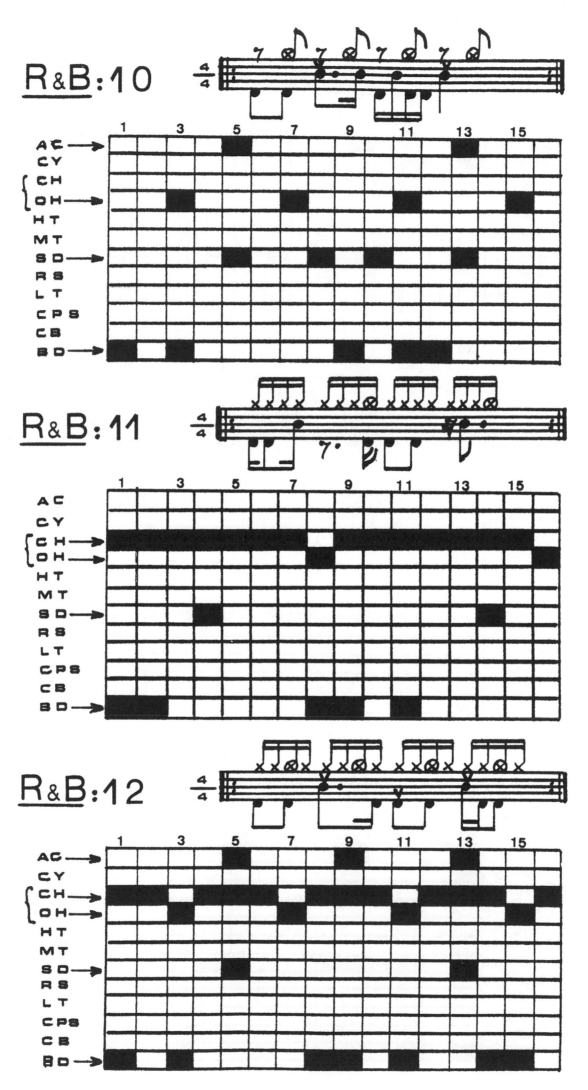

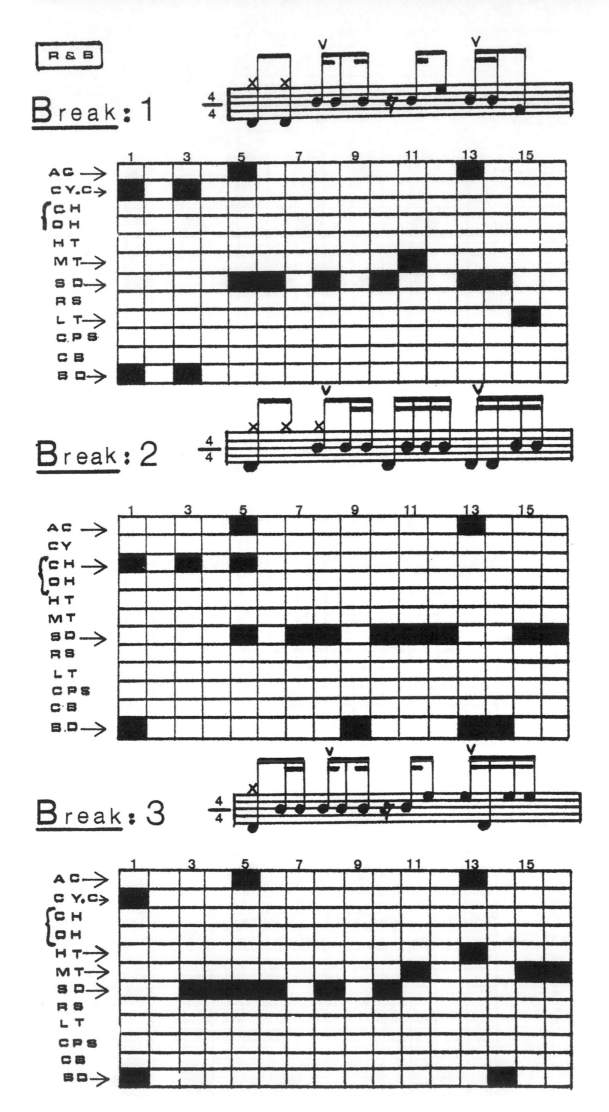

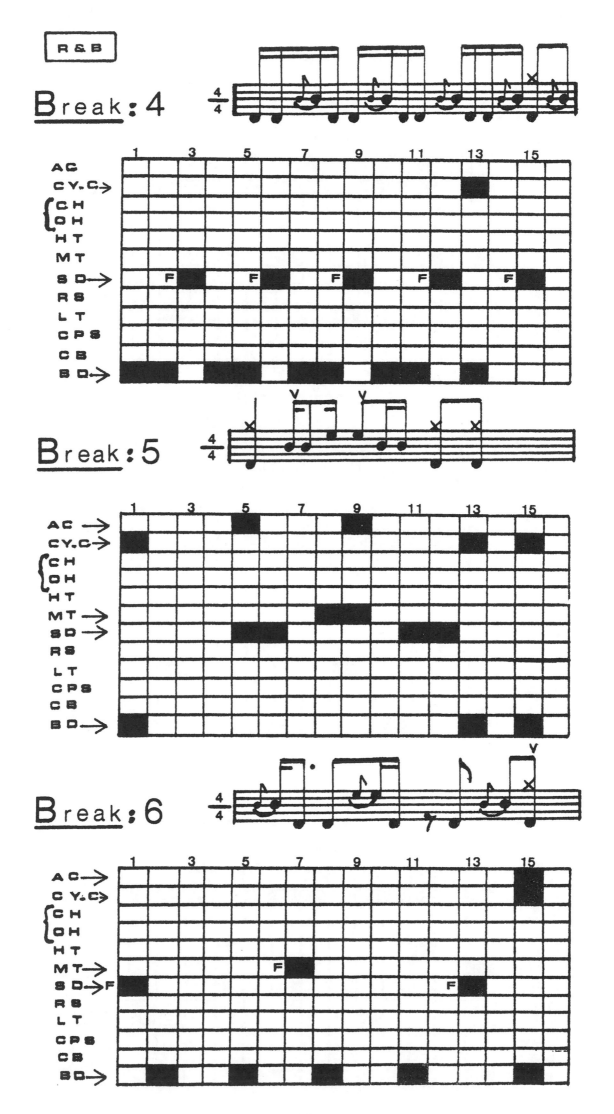

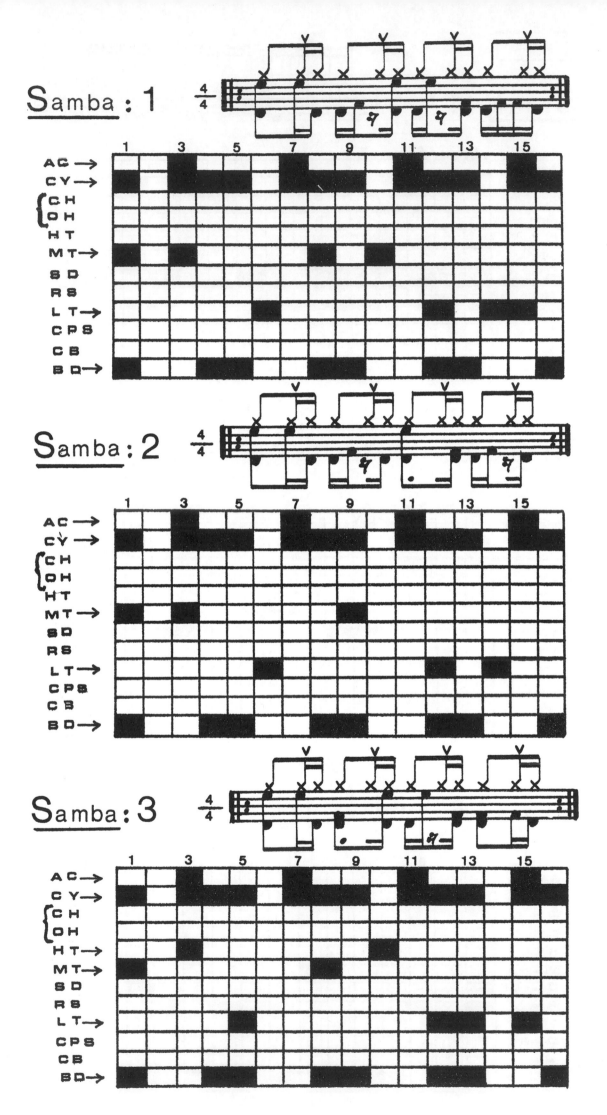

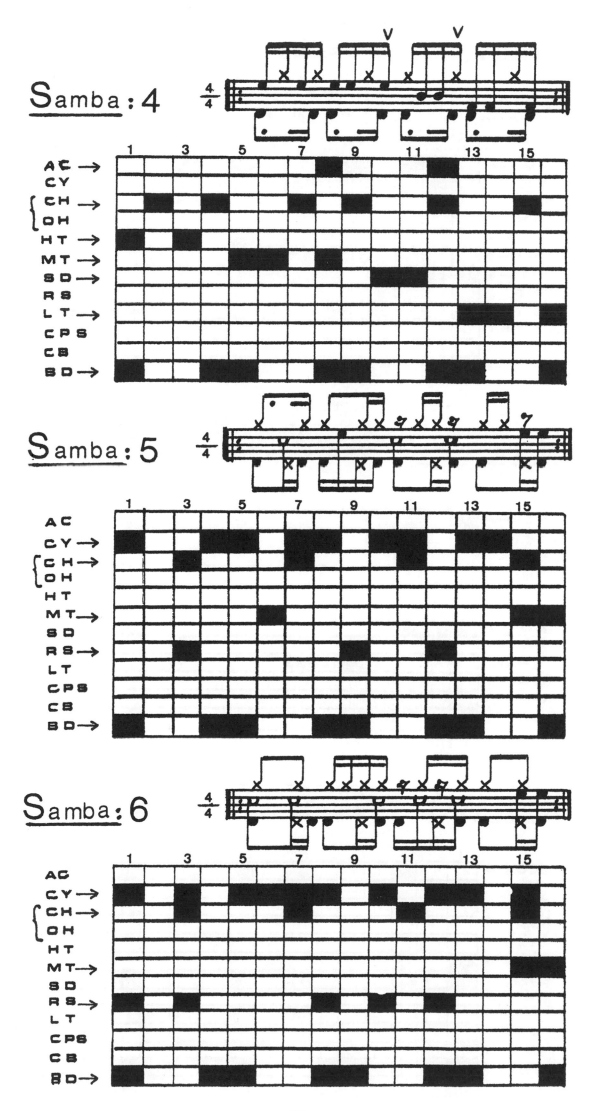

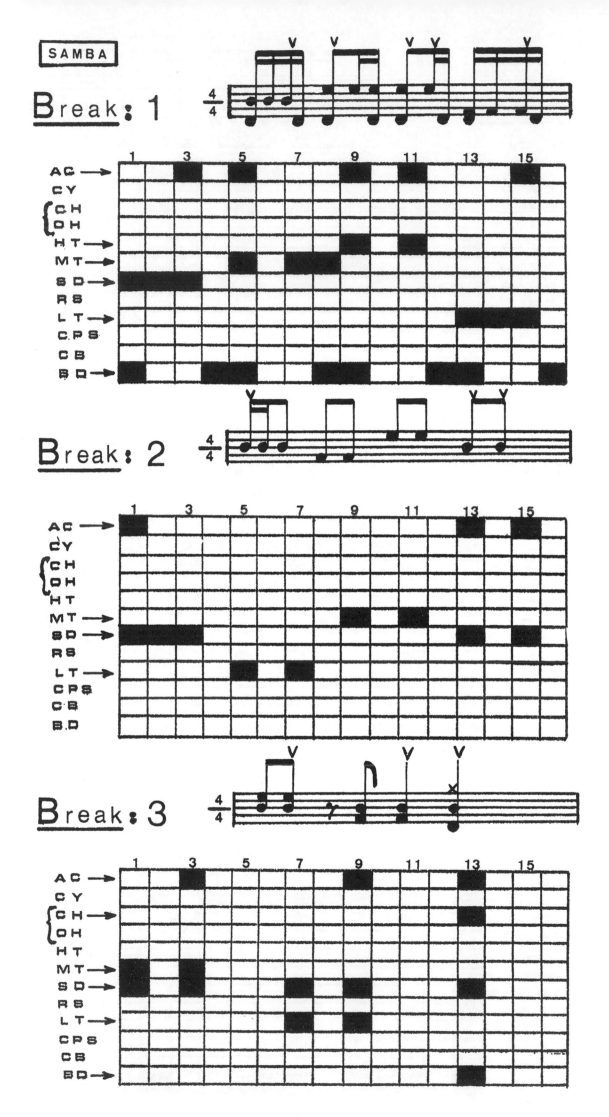

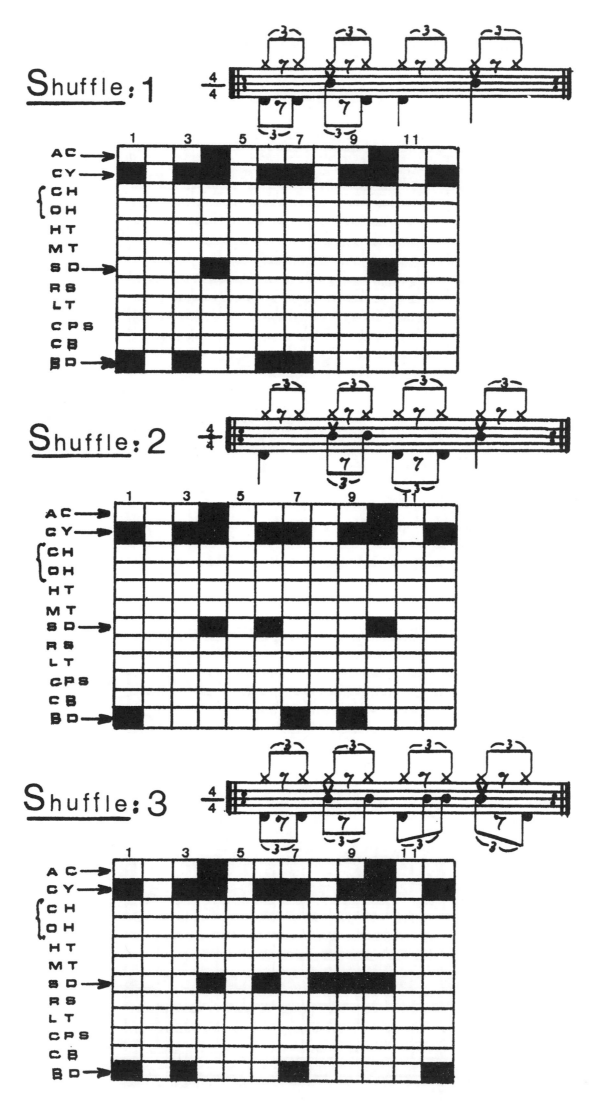

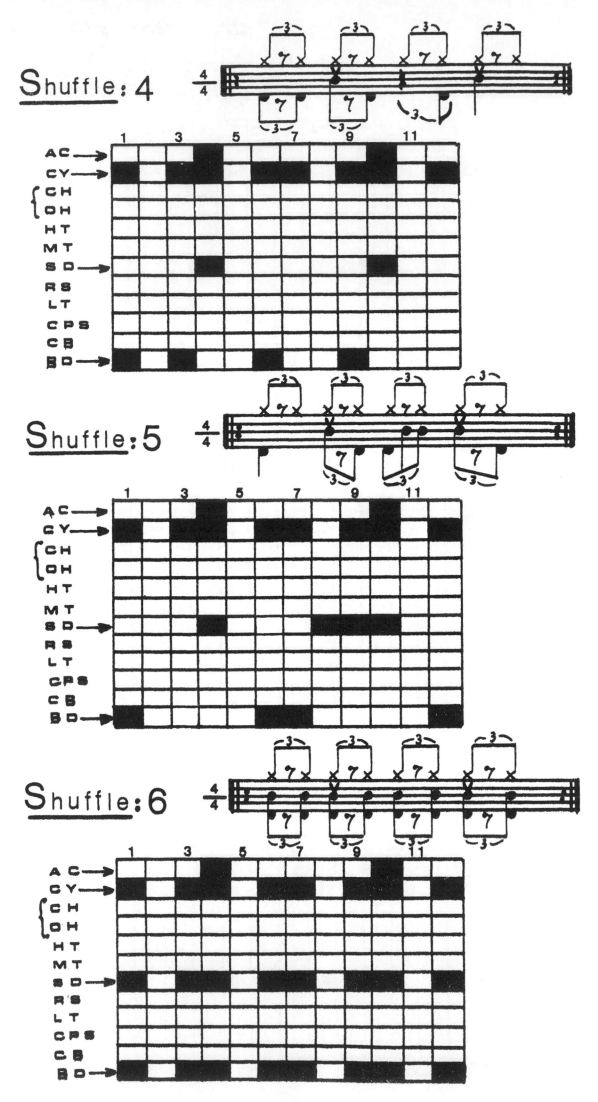

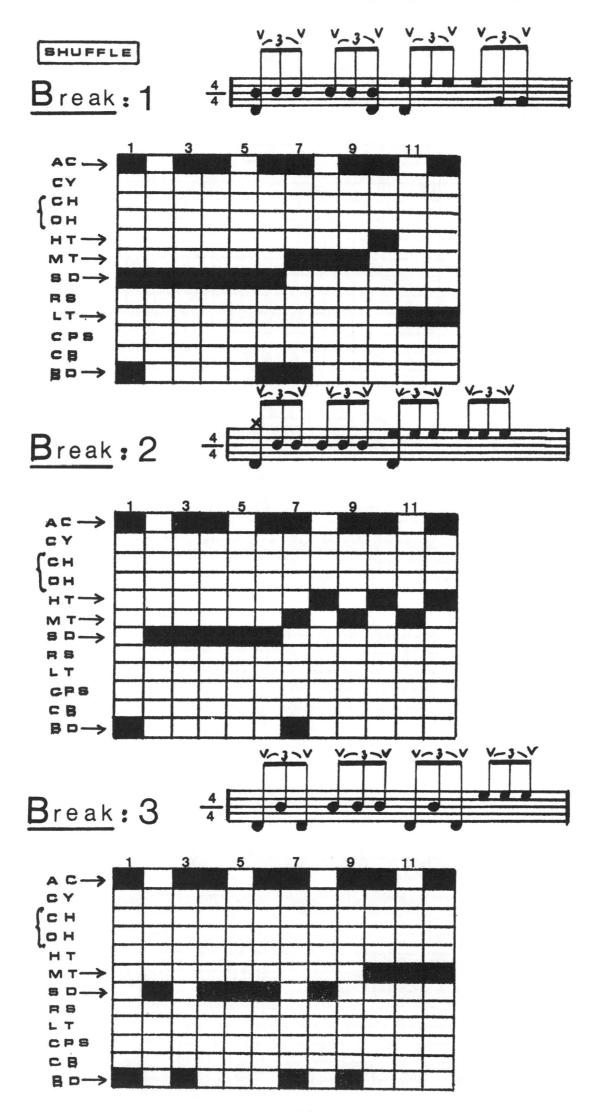

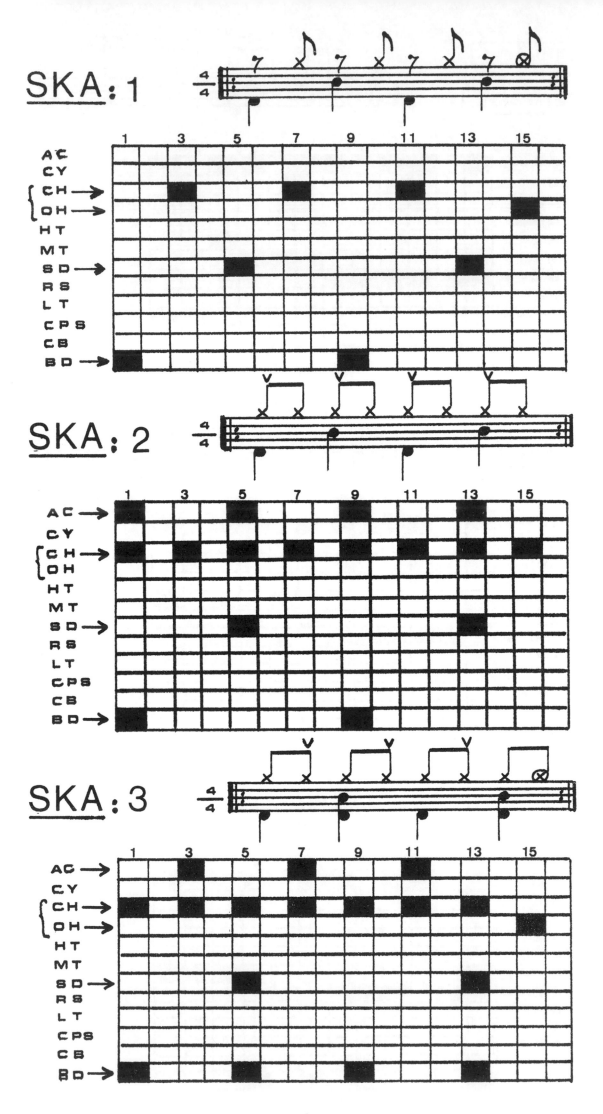

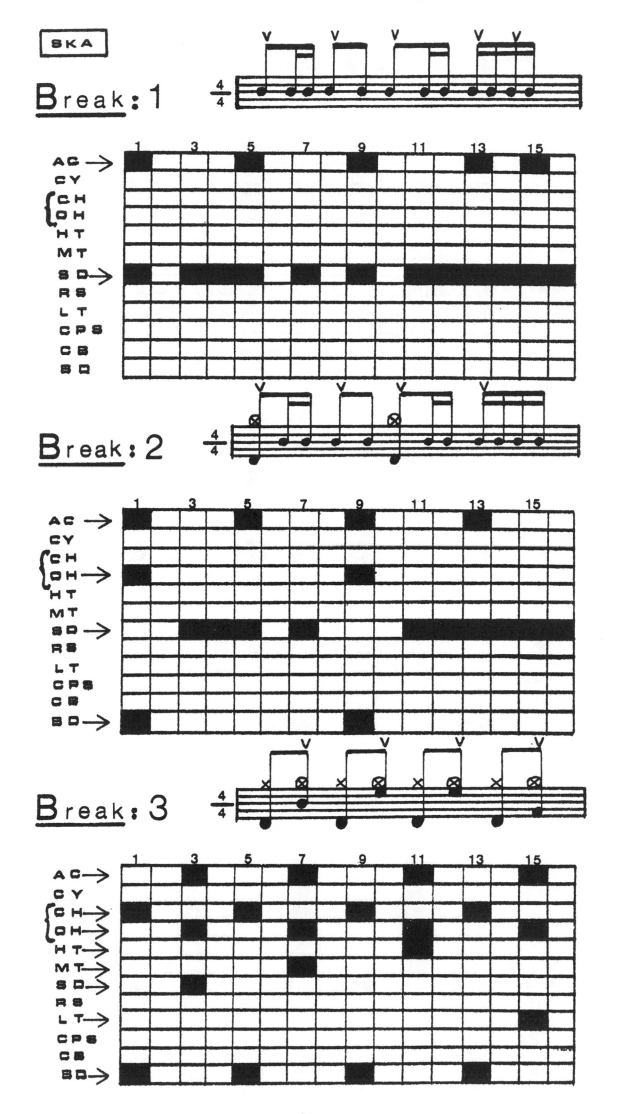

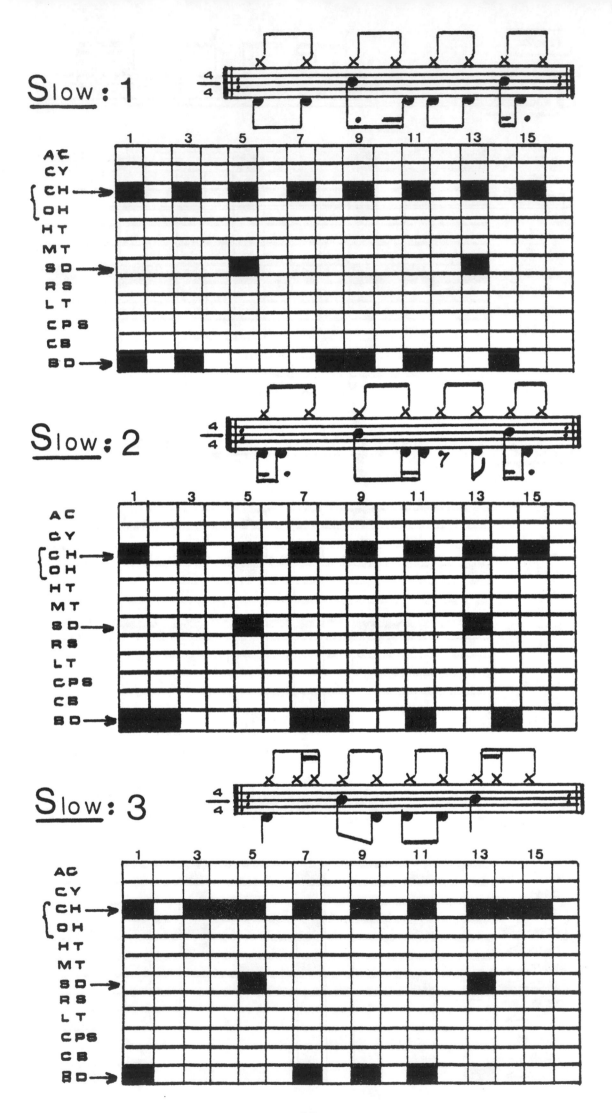

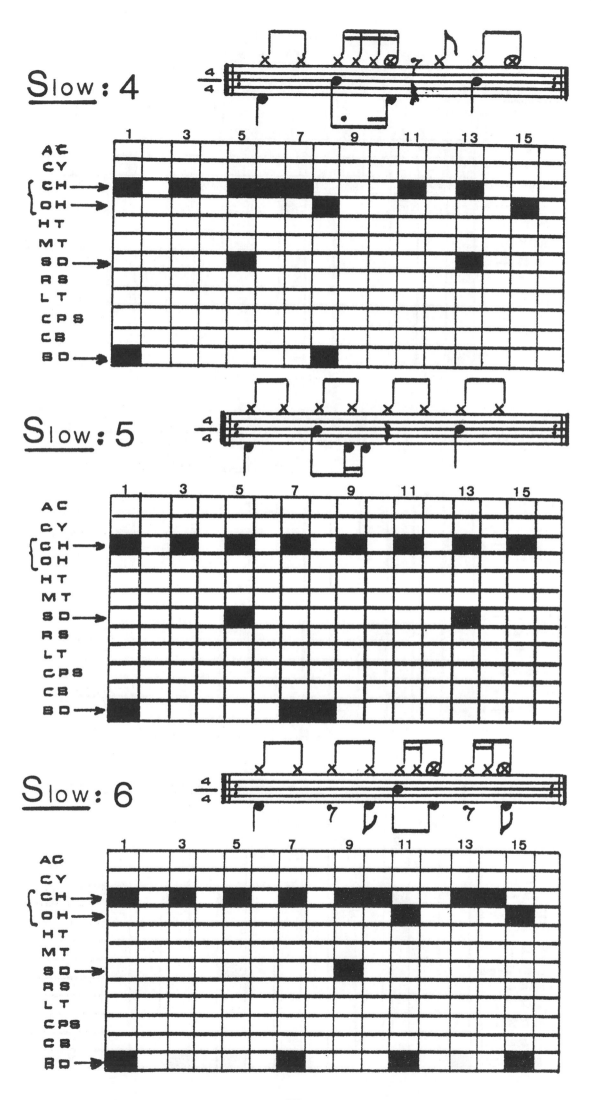

83

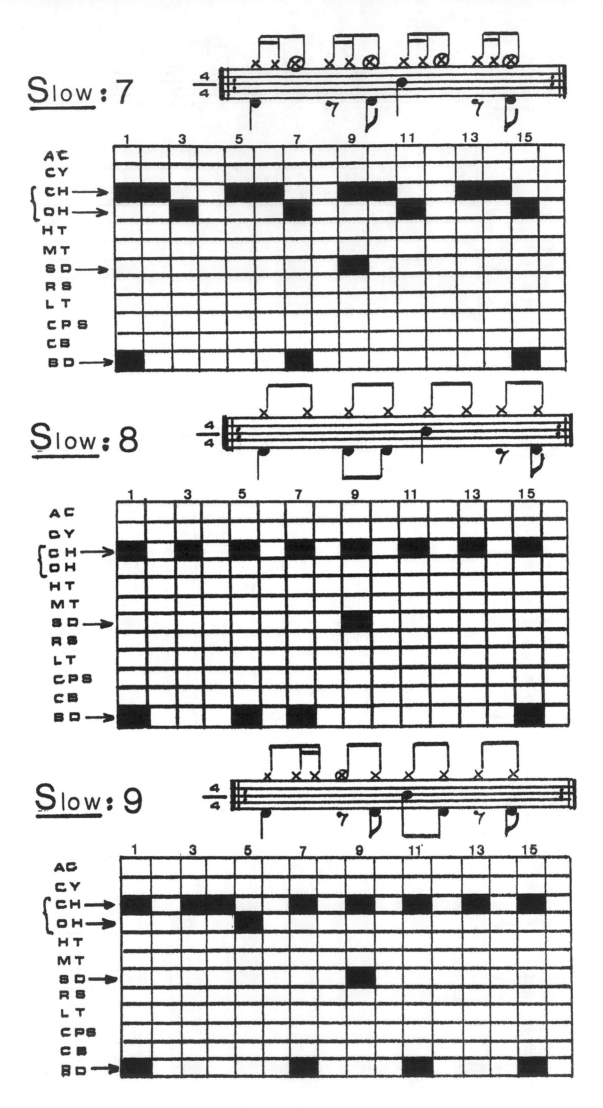

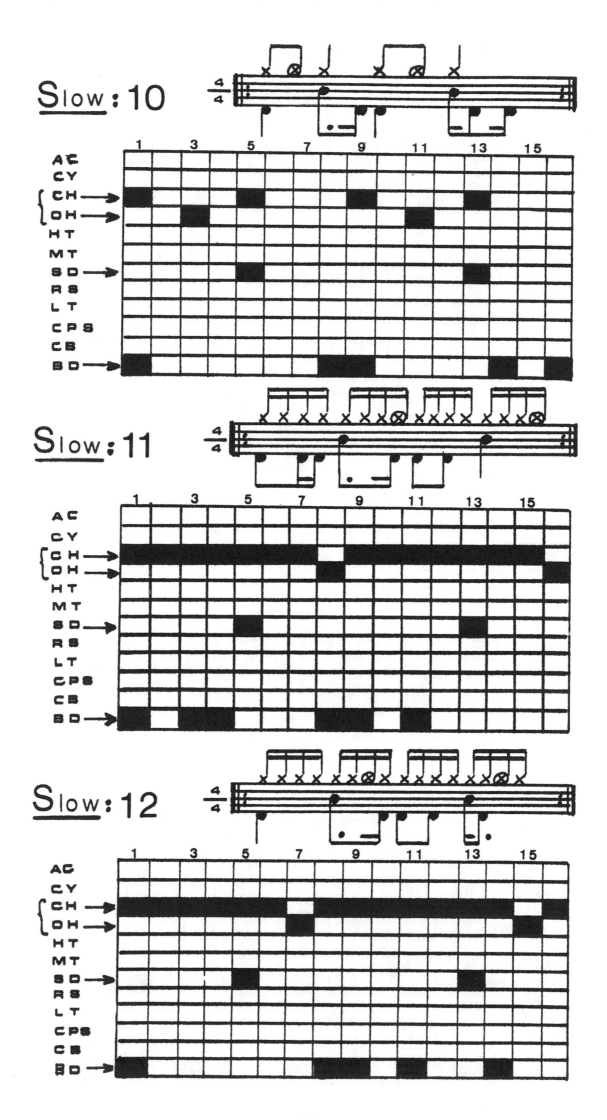

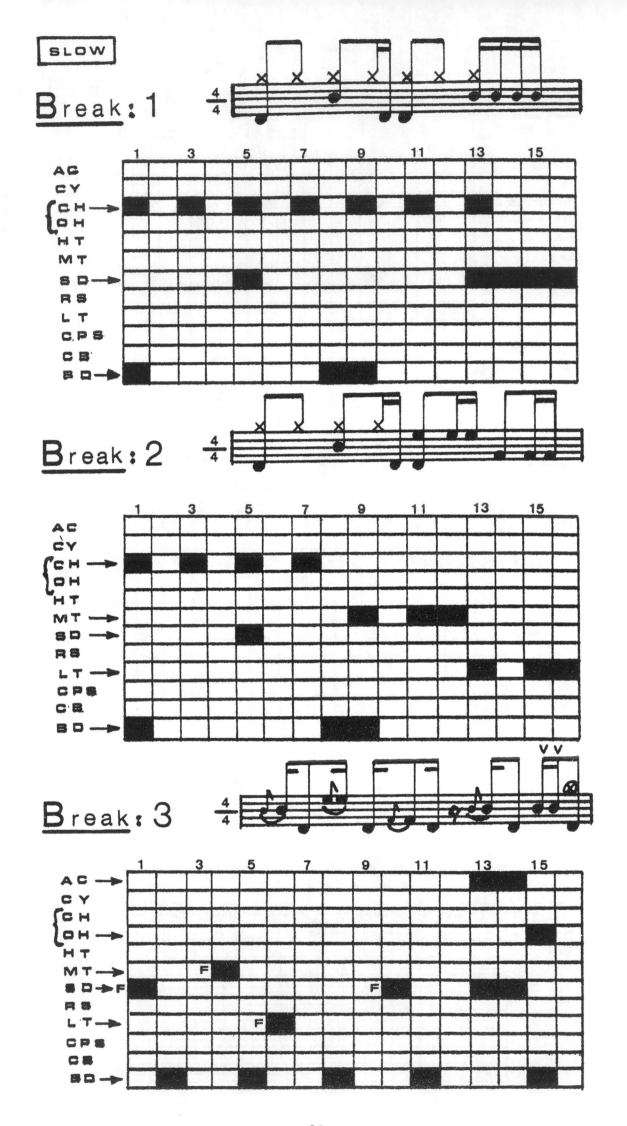

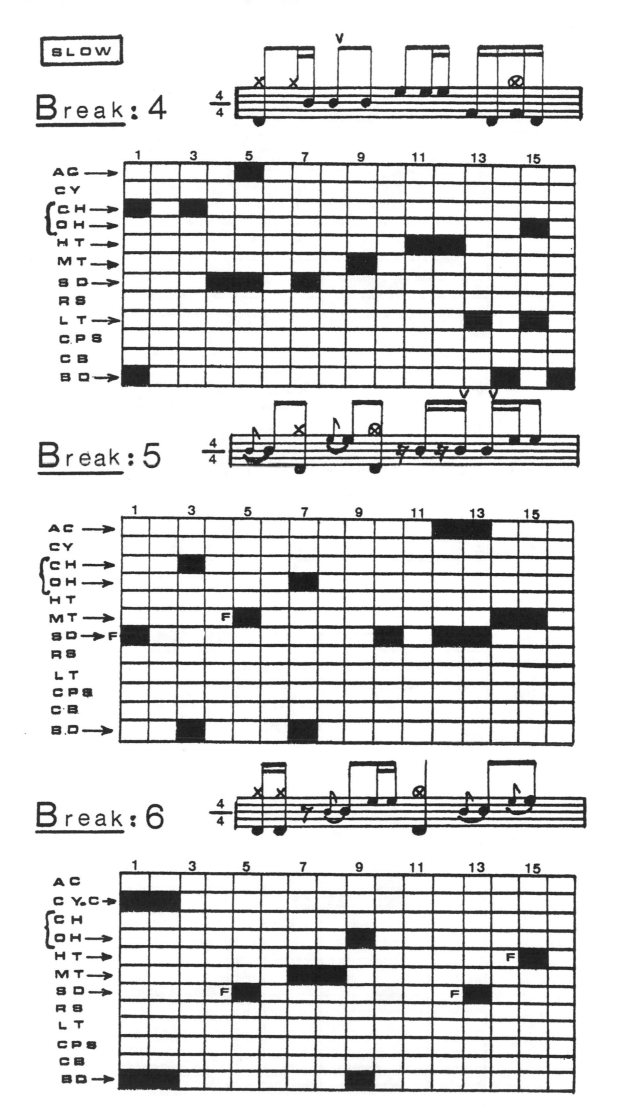

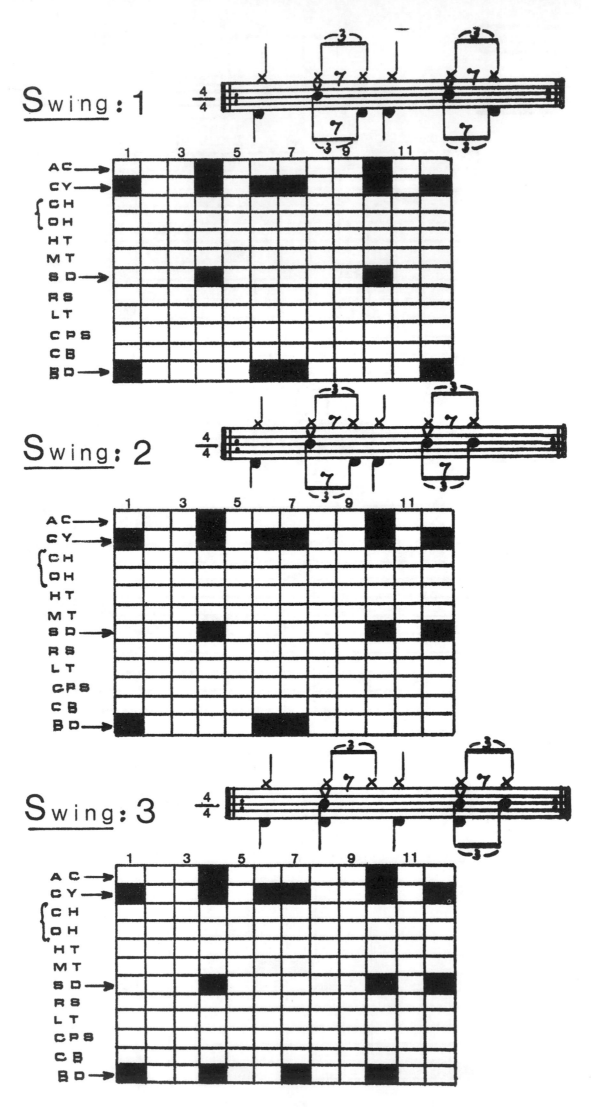

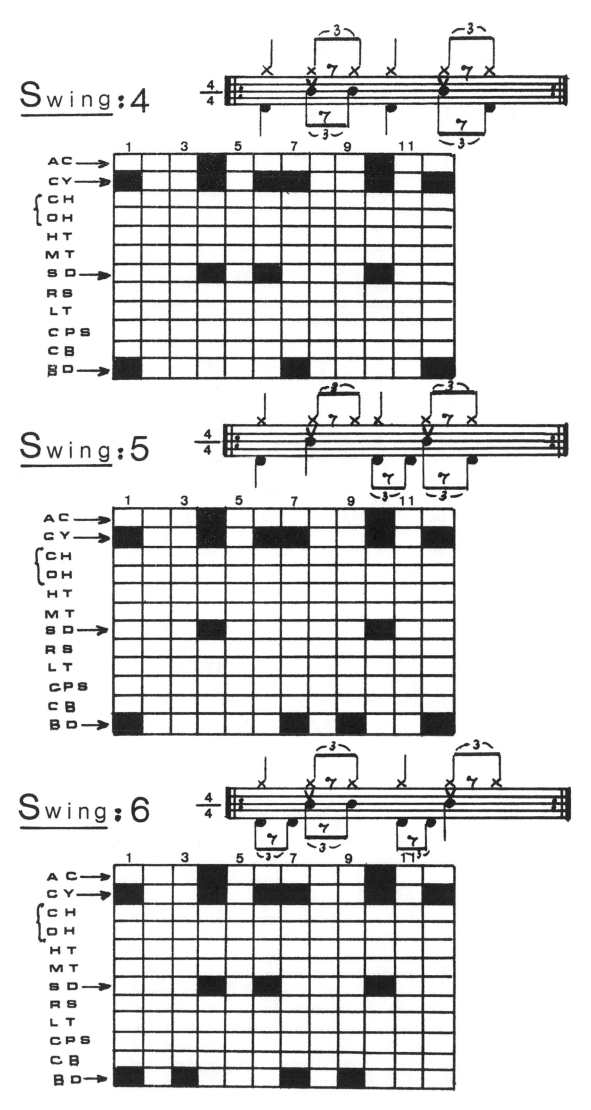

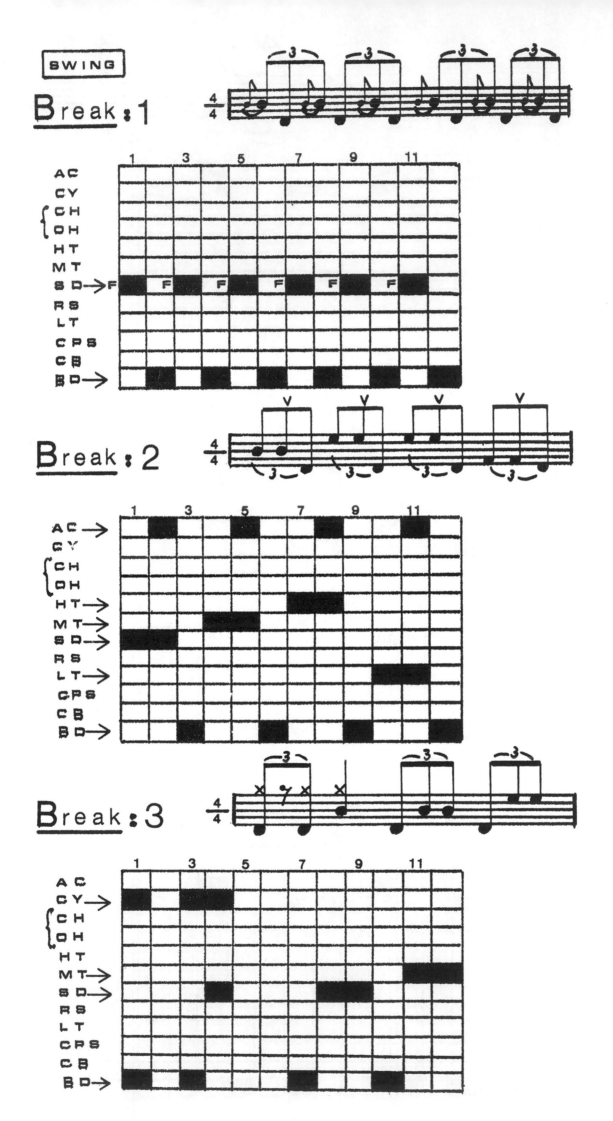

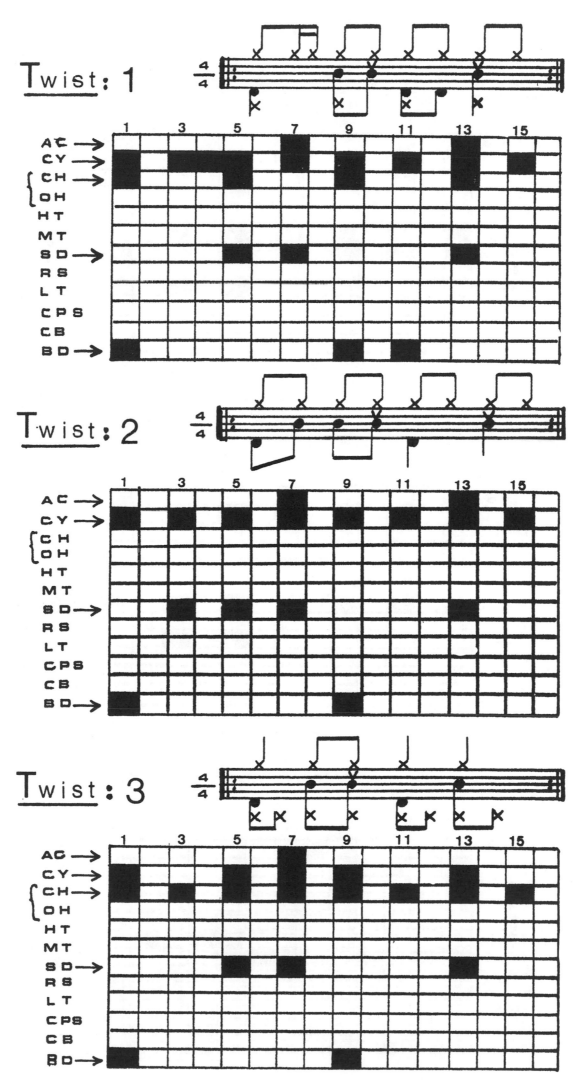

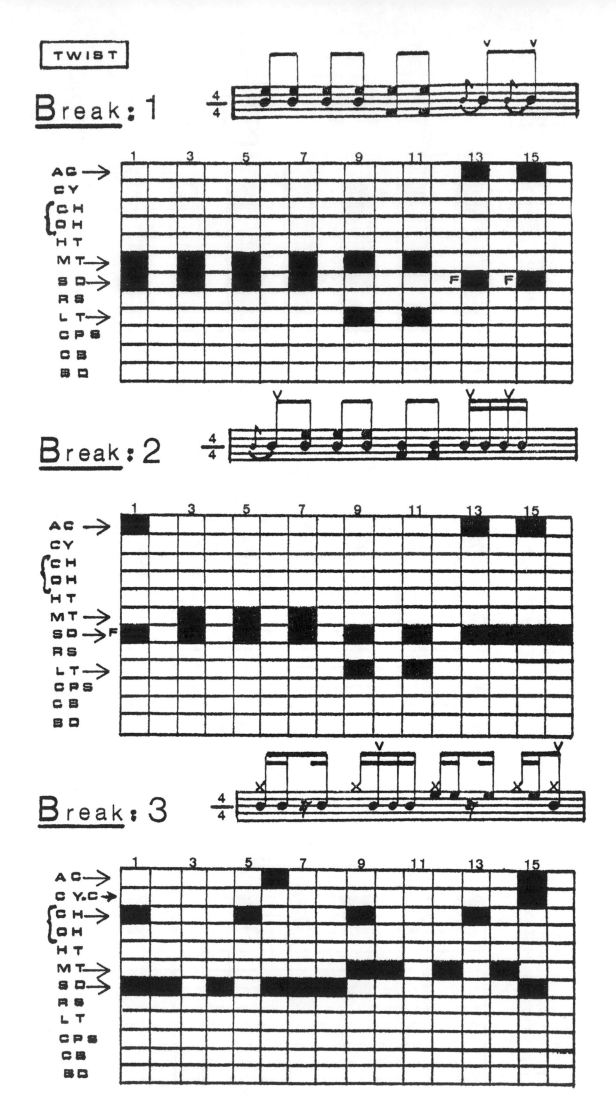

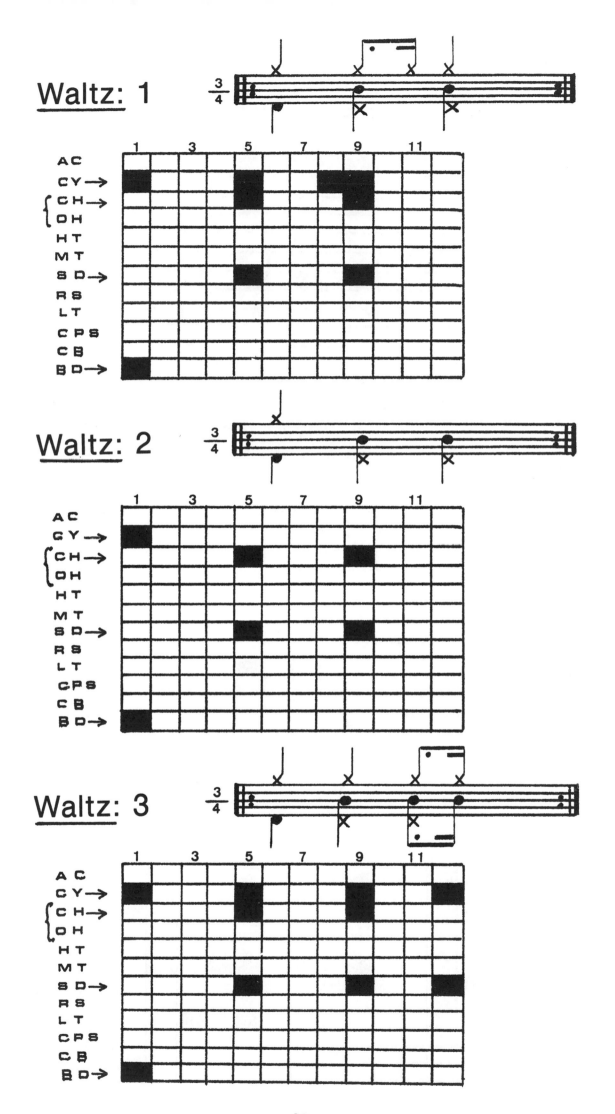

93

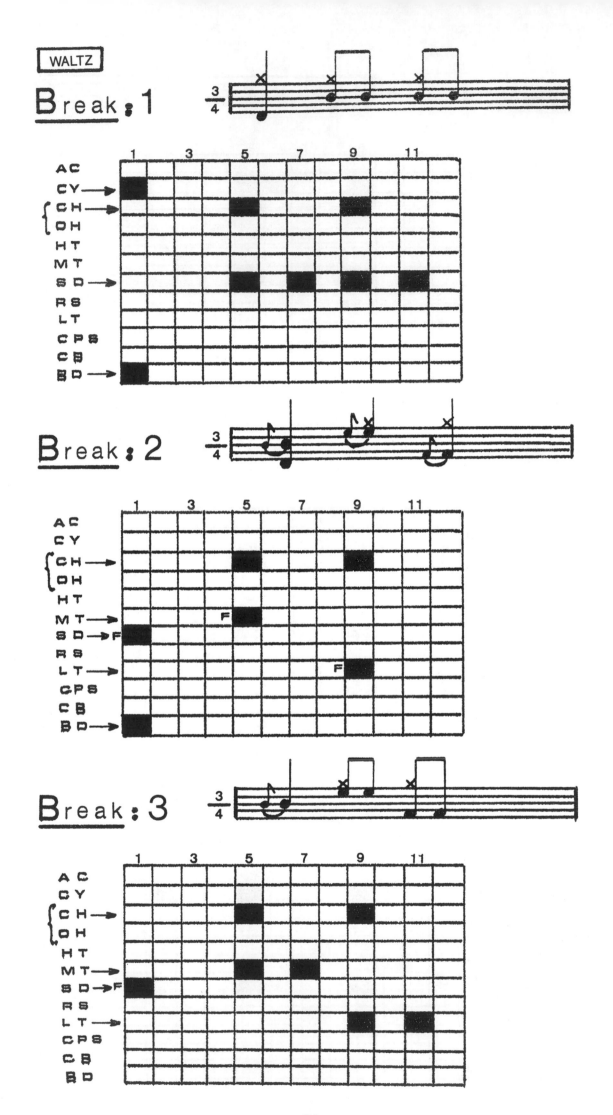

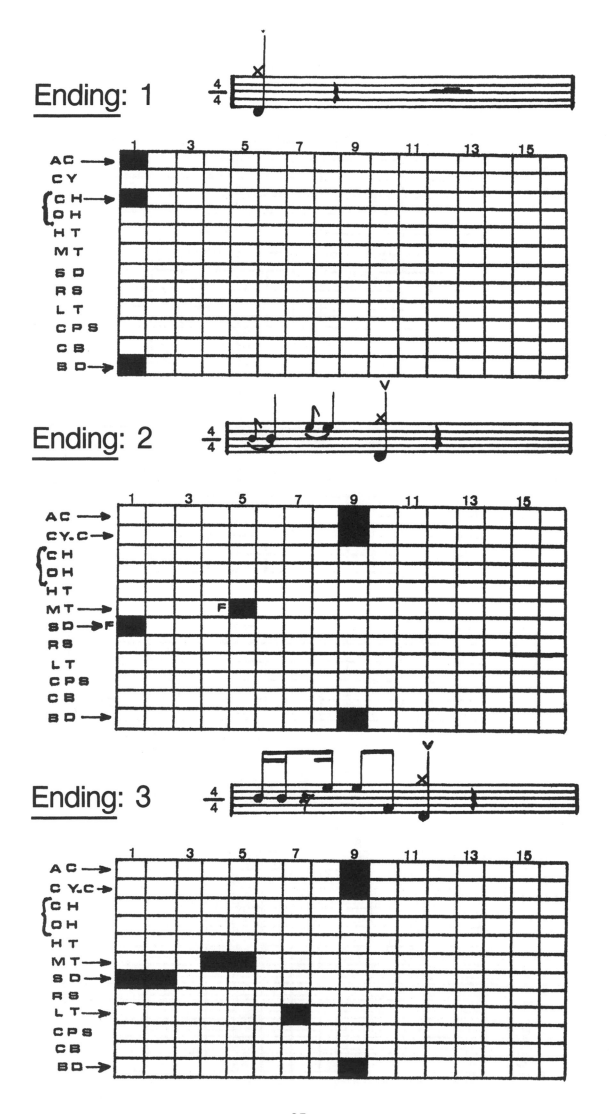

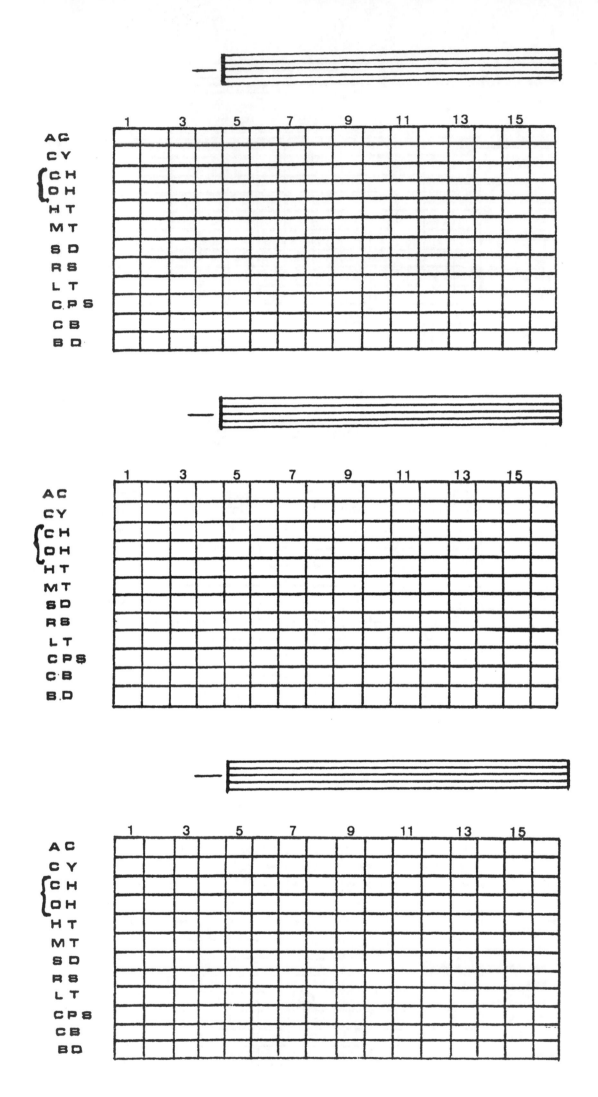